Leicestershire

GENERAL EDITOR: AIDAN CHAM

War at sea

Here are fourteen true stories written by the men who lived through the experiences they describe of the war at sea during the Second World War. They describe battles above and below the waves. The great warships *Scharnhorst* – pride of the German navy – and HMS *Duke of York* slog it out to the death. Convoys of merchant ships brave the U-boats, their all-too-few escort vessels fighting desperately to beat the undersea menace. These are the kinds of story you will discover in this book: stories that tell tales of courage and human endurance during the ghastly years of world-wide conflict.

Other Topliners compiled by Aidan Chambers include:
Fighters in the sky
Men at war

TOPLINERS

War at sea

Compiled by
Aidan Chambers

Macmillan

Selection © Aidan Chambers 1978

All rights reserved. No part of this publication
may be reproduced or transmitted, in any form
or by any means, without permission.

Published in *Topliners* in 1978 by
MACMILLAN EDUCATION LTD
Houndmills Basingstoke Hampshire RG21 2XS
and London
Associated companies in Delhi Dublin
Hong Kong Johannesburg Lagos Melbourne
New York Singapore and Tokyo

Printed in Great Britain by
Cox & Wyman Ltd
London, Reading and Fakenham

Topliners are sold subject to the condition that they
shall not, by way of trade or otherwise, be lent, resold,
hired out or otherwise circulated without the publisher's
prior consent in any form of binding or cover other than
that in which they are published, and without a condition,
including this condition, being imposed on the
subsequent purchaser.

Contents

1. Dunkirk *Richard Collier* 1
2. Teach you to drown, young 'un *Ronald Healiss* 8
3. Save Our Souls *Elspeth Huxley* 15
4. Contact ... contact *Donald MacIntyre* 19
5. The end of an era *O'Dowd Gallagher* 25
6. The sauciest job since Drake *Donald MacIntyre* 35
7. Battling through to Malta *Hugh Popham, Arthur Thorpe and Anthony Kimmins* 54
8. Submarine 'Wahoo' *Donald MacIntyre* 63
9. Midgets attack giants *Godfrey Place* 73
10. The 'Scharnhorst' has been sunk! *B. B. Ramsden* 82
11. D-Day *William Pugsley and Denis Glover* 91
12. Attack! *Edward Young* 109
13. Suicide pilots *Officers of HMS 'Formidable'* 114
14. Surrender *Anthony Kimmins* 117

Acknowledgements

The author and publishers wish to thank the following who have kindly given permission for the use of copyright material.

Beaverbrook Newspapers Ltd for the report in *The Daily Express*, 12 December 1941, by O'Dowd Gallagher;

William Blackwood and Sons Ltd for an extract from *The Sinking of the Scharnhorst* by B. B. Ramsden;

Chatto and Windus Ltd and Mrs Elspeth Huxley for an extract from *Atlantic Ordeal: Mary Cornish*;

William Collins, Sons & Co. Ltd for the extract from *The Sands of Dunkirk* by Richard Collier;

Rupert Crew Ltd on behalf of Ronald Healiss for the extract from *Adventure Glorious*, published by Frederick Muller Ltd;

The Daily Telegraph Ltd for an article by Arthur Thorpe, 14 August 1942;

Evans Brothers Ltd for extracts from *Fighting Ships and Seamen* and *Fighting Under the Sea* by Donald MacIntyre;

John Farquharson Ltd on behalf of W. R. Fell for the extract from *The Sea Our Shield*;

Edward Young for the extract from *One of our Submarines* published by Hart-Davis, MacGibbon Ltd (1952);

David Higham Associates for the extracts from *Half Time* (1947) and *The Listener* 27 August 1942, both by Anthony Kimmins;

Lt-Cdr Denis Glover for an extract from *It Was D-Day*;

Hugh Popham for the extract from *Sea Flight* (1954) first published by William Kimber & Co. Ltd;

Seeley, Service and Cooper Ltd for extracts from *U-Boat Killer* by Donald MacIntyre, and *A Formidable Commission* by the Wardroom Officers of HMS *Formidable*.

The publishers regret that they have been unable to trace the copyright owner in one particular case, and apologise if the copyright has unwittingly been infringed.

1 Dunkirk

Richard Collier

The Second World War began, for Britain, on 3 September 1939. By May 1940 the British army in France was on the brink of a disastrous defeat. Hitler's well-equipped troops were storming towards the English Channel pushing before them 400 000 Allied soldiers, whose fate seemed to be either capture or death at Dunkirk.

But the Prime Minister, Winston Churchill, had a rescue plan. All available seaworthy boats, from small family pleasure cruisers a few metres in length to destroyers of the Royal Navy, were gathered together in the English south coast ports and prepared for a journey to France. On 27 May this motley fleet set out, the strangest armada ever seen in the history of the world, its mission, many people thought, hopeless from the start. While it sailed the notoriously dangerous Channel, the battered and weary British army waited on the Dunkirk sands. By 4 June, when the Germans at last took the town, this courageous fleet had brought home 338 226 men.

In his book *The Sands of Dunkirk* Richard Collier described some of the boats and their makeshift crews.

Now from every port the boats were moving out, bent on a crazy, incredible rescue ... from Ramsgate and Margate ... from Dover, Folkestone and Portsmouth ... from Sheerness and down the tidal rivers ... their wakes planing like a sickle through wet grass ... frail streamers of smoke trailing to the sky ... a fleet almost a thousand strong.

There never had been an armada like it. The destroyer *Harvester*, built to fulfil a foreign contract, with all its gun-laying instructions in Brazilian; the *Count Dracula*, launch of the German Admiral Ludwig von Reuter, scuttled at

Scapa Flow in 1919 but salvaged years later; the armed yacht *Grive*, where the captain, the Hon. Lionel Lambert, took his own personal chef; the *Canterbury*, the bejewelled ferry-boat of the cross-Channel run with memories of Princess Paul of Yugoslavia and Delysia; Arthur Dench's *Letitia*, the little green cockle-boat from the Essex mudflats, breasting the waves like a seagull.

And still they streamed across the waters: the Thames hopper barge *Galleon's Reach*, built to pack in not men but the muddy spoil of dredgers; Tom Sopwith's yacht *Endeavour*; the Fleetwood fishing trawler *Jacinta*, reeking of cod; the Yangtse gunboat *Mosquito* bristling with armament to ward off Chinese river pirates; *Reiger*, a Dutch *schuit*, redolent of onions, still hung with geranium pots, with mighty bunks for mighty men; the Deal beach boat *Dumpling*, built in Napoleon's time, with a skipper seventy years young.

As the cockleshell armada fanned out towards Dunkirk, even seasoned naval officers felt a lump rise to their throats: absurd yet magnificent, it was without all precedent in the world's naval history. On the bridge of the destroyer *Malcolm*, the navigating officer, Lieutenant Ian Cox, was moved almost to tears to see the oncoming fleet led by, of all craft, the *Wootton*, the old Isle of Wight car ferry, wallowing like a sawn-off landing stage through the water. His voice shaken by emotion, Cox burst out to the seaman beside him with the classic lines of Shakespeare's *Henry V* before another assault upon the coast of France:

> And gentlemen in England now a-bed
> Shall think themselves accurs'd they were not here,
> And hold their manhoods cheap while any speaks
> That fought with us upon Saint Crispin's day.

As with the boats, so with the crews. The rich and the famous, the poor and the unknown, as motley a bunch as ever set sail made up this mercy fleet. The Earl of Craven, third engineer in the rescue tug *St Olave* ... a Dominican monk in a reefer jersey skippering the yacht *Gulzar* ... 'George', the salty bos'n of the contraband control vessel *Ocean Breeze*, still wearing a privateer's golden earrings below his steel helmet ... Captain 'Potato' Jones, sixty-seven-year-old skipper of the *Marie Llewellyn*, famed for running Franco's blockade through the Spanish Civil War.

Age was no barrier: though skipper Charlie Alexander didn't know it yet, fourteen-year-old Ronald Pridmore, the galley boy, was sheltering below deck in the tug *Sun IV*, determined to show there were other proofs of manhood than shaving. Lieutenant-Colonel Charles Wharton, coming down from Oulton Broad in Suffolk, felt the same: they had rejected him for re-enlistment at sixty, but still, though wearing carpet slippers for comfort, he'd show them this was an oldster's war too.

Neither race nor colour had meaning, for this was an international fleet – a true United Nations ... Californian-born John Fernald skippering one of the twelve lifeboats towed by the tug *Racia* ... Dick Jacobus Hoogerbeets, a young shipyard plater from Ijmuiden, aboard motorboat 74 ... Chinese Steward Ah Fong rushing tea to Captain Lewes on the bridge of *Bideford* ... a crew from Stornoway with their own Gaelic interpreter in the minesweeper *Fitzroy* ... Fireman Ali Khan, shovelling as if all life depended on it in the stokehold of *Dorrien Rose*.

The mood was unique too – the grim gaiety of the gambler staking all his chips on the last spin of the wheel. Bouncing towards Dunkirk in motorboat 67, a First World War veteran with a compass twenty degrees out, Lieutenant Courtney Anderson RN, almost carolled with joy; only a bottle of malted-milk tablets donated by his mother-in-law stood between the crew and starvation, but today it was good to be alive.

Spotting an old friend, Lieutenant Chris Dreyer, ferrying a brigadier back from Dunkirk in motorboat 102, Anderson couldn't resist yelling: 'Excuse me, can you tell me the way to Dunkirk?'

Dreyer, playing up, jerked a thumb: 'Back there, you can't miss it. It's burning.' As the brigadier turned crimson with horror, both skippers collapsed in unholy glee.

Not all the outsiders had signed T 124 – the form that made them Royal Naval volunteers for a month – for they prized their independence too much. Some in any case were there despite official qualms: Stewardess Amy Goodrich, the only woman to be awarded a Dunkirk decoration, swore that so long as the nurses sailed in the hospital ship *Dinard* she'd sail too. Most were entitled to £3 for their services, but few bothered to collect. They were sworn to one single improbable purpose: the rescue of the British army.

Their callings were as varied as their garb. Engineer Fred Reynard, who'd talked an admiral into letting his crew take over the motor vessel *Bee*, wore an open-necked shirt, V-necked sweater, blue dungarees. Wilfred Pym Trotter, a Bank of England clerk, wore much the same, though he'd reported as for any city stint – bowler hat, pin-stripe trousers, umbrella. Dr Basil Smith, a peppery little chartered accountant who skippered the *Constant Nymph*, wore a padded golf cap, a lounge suit and a cork life-belt so thick he had to stand a foot away from the wheel. Raphael de Sola, one of London's wealthiest stockbrokers, wore the full rig of the Royal London Yacht Club: blue gabardine raincoat lined with red flannel, yachting cap with the club's insignia.

Aboard the *Tollesbury*, Skipper Lemon Webb was garbed more prosaically: old sailcloth trousers and jersey, shapeless trilby hat still perched on his head. He wasn't dressing up for this show.

Incredibly, the old barge was as well equipped as any craft destined to make this trip. Despite Captain Wharton's efforts at Ramsgate, despite all that Rear-Admiral Alfred Taylor, *Dynamo*'s maintenance officer at Sheerness, could do, craft after craft was moving out with scarcely enough gear or provisions for a leisurely cruise up an estuary.

Aboard the motor yacht *Constant Nymph*, Dr Basil Smith and two stoker ratings were already off Dunkirk – ferrying load after load of French troops to the Dutch *schuit Jutland*. The excitement staved off hunger, which was as well – the Navy had given them a sirloin of beef and a sack of potatoes but the little boat boasted only a two-burner primus.

In the Clacton lifeboat Wilfred Pym Trotter faced the same problem. There was just one way to make tea: wedge a kettleful of water, tea and milk in the boat's funnel and wait until the dubious brew boiled.

It was the same in boat after boat. From the Admiralty's Small Vessels Pool to Ramsay's own staff, the Navy had worked like beavers to muster the small craft at all. Boat-builders Jack Powell and his brother Pat had been two of a team working non-stop at Sheerness to make the craft serviceable – in the grim knowledge that a full forty per cent had never put to sea.

Now, *en route* for Dunkirk, both Powells saw the shape of things to come. In the motor yacht *Reda* the engine control gave out before Dover was even lost to view; thereafter Pat Powell's petty officer had to work the old remote-control engine by hand. In the twin-engined *Cordelia* Jack Powell was at his wits' end: the cabin-cruiser was leaking at the seams and only one engine deigned to function at all.

And the small craft under naval control fared no better. Sub-Lieutenant Alfred Weaver had no sooner left Ramsgate than the *Quijijana*'s engine caught fire; dousing it with the extinguisher, Weaver ploughed on, but the minute he sighted Dunkirk the old yellow-funnelled pleasure launch began shipping water. Finding the bilge pump inoperative, Weaver and his crew had to bale desperately with their service caps.

For the first time Weaver saw the brass plate affixed to the bulwarks – 'Licensed to ply between Chertsey and Teddington' – and understood. That stretch of the river Thames, he knew, measured only fourteen miles.

The armament was primitive. Aboard the yacht *Chrystobel II*, a rich man's plaything, Lieutenant Hubert Wigfull had one Lewis gun – but the only sturdier weapon was an

1890 saluting gun geared to an angle of forty-five degrees. And other ships, moving out with less protection, faced a grimmer ordeal. The cargo boat *Roebuck*, still on the Channel Islands run, had been unloading daffodils and new potatoes in Weymouth Harbour when the order came to set out. The old ship wasn't even degaussed – her hull wound with electric cable as protection against magnetic mines – yet Captain Wilfred Larbalestier moved off without question.

In the personnel ship *St Helier* Captain Richard Pitman had no contact with the outside world at all; after several gruelling trips twenty of his crew had walked out so that now, halfway to Dunkirk, he didn't even have a wireless operator. After a despairing prowl round the wireless cabin, Pitman, sending for engineer Dick Dougal and second mate Frank Martin, experimentally touched a switch. Promptly a blue flame danced like a will o' the wisp across the cabin; the three men gave up. Without benefit of radio the *St Helier* steamed on.

The pitiful shortages might have made any man lose heart. In the tug *Sun IV* the 'ample supplies' of dressings promised to Charles Jackson's Gravesend ambulance team just hadn't been forthcoming: even the surgical scissors turned out to be nail scissors. Without more ado they stripped off their underclothes, began slicing them into bandages. Not to be outdone, skipper Charlie Alexander rummaged through cupboards and drawers. Soon all of them were shearing methodically through towels, pillowcases, even the skipper's shirts.

Now the small craft drew nearer to the shore. The full impact of Dunkirk plunged home.

Above the scene for thirty miles loomed the black pall of the oiltanks of St Pol, 11 000 feet high, a mile wide, two million tons of oil roaring as one. To Chief Engineer George Tooley, aboard the *Maid of Orleans*, it looked 'like doom itself'.

A few found grounds for optimism. Glancing at the inky

smoke that mingled with the fog, almost blotting out the land, ambulance officer Charles Jackson, in *Sun IV*, felt his spirits soaring: 'Good old Navy, look at the smokescreen they've put up.'

2 Teach you to drown, young 'un

Ronald Healiss

For Britain June 1940 was the worst month of the entire war. Dunkirk was taken on the fourth, leaving Hitler master of Europe and poised ready to pounce on Britain itself. His navy was gaining confidence and strength daily. German U-boats were attacking British merchantmen, sinking vital supplies from America. And the huge pocket battleships, the pride of Hitler's brand-new fleet, were threatening to blockade Britain completely, cutting her off from all outside aid.

On 9 June the aircraft carrier HMS *Glorious* was steaming home from Norway, where the British army was in retreat and being evacuated from its last foothold against the Germans. *Glorious* was short of fuel and hardly prepared for battle. Not a good time, if there ever was a good time, to be caught by two of Hitler's battleships, the *Scharnhorst* and *Gneisenau*. *Glorious* was taken by surprise when the two giants opened fire on her at 4.30 p.m. An hour and a half later *Glorious* turned turtle and sank. She was another grievous loss to the Royal Navy at a time when Britain could ill afford such a disaster.

Ronald Healiss was a marine aboard the carrier at the time. In *Adventure Glorious* he gave his account of the attack, and of the experience of being cast adrift from a stricken warship, an experience thousands of men were to live through in the six years of the war.

I reckon we were making nearly thirty knots, and *Glorious* was shuddering with speed. But I didn't know it. I was thinking. Ugly thoughts they were. Come to think of it, there must have been a lot of a rowdy jumble going on, because there was so much thudding of machinery, and the cutting of the wind, and the shouting of brisk orders that we hardly heard the first salvo above it. You got so used to this conglomeration of sounds in the *Glorious* you didn't notice they were going on . . . until the crash of a shell put your familiar rhythm out of tempo, and there was all this noise at once, hitting you with its stark ugliness.

The flight deck above us was wreathed in smoke, then tongues of flame, then the staccato sounds of fire rose to a great roar, and a red wall like a living furnace rose from the hangar well.

Then it came again, like distant thunder, culminating in a sudden wall of vicious sound, leaving the whole gun platform shuddering with the impact. Merciful God, they'd got their range right! . . .

I looked up the cliff face of the wall of steel forward of the bridge and saw the steel shattering. Plummets of smoke filled the air as I watched in horror. They'd hit the bridge. At the impact, I threw myself on the platform instinctively.

We waited on maybe a couple of minutes.

'This is bloody silly!' shouted Ginger above the roar of flames. 'There's nothing we can do here. Let's scram up and do what we can about the hangar fire.'

'But orders . . .' said Taff stolidly, shaking his head.

'There won't be any more orders. Not from there. The bridge is gone.'

The rest couldn't hear this above the roar of the inferno; but they could read Ginger's lips, and we were with him. No use staying here.

It was that instant another salvo hit, and the whole side of the *Glorious* seemed to cave in, leaving a choking cloud of smoke and a thunderous roar that echoed away to the darkening sky. The sea, so calm before the action, was now churned up and flecked with grey. God, I thought, we've nearly had our chips! Stupefied, we waited. And I wish we hadn't. For that's when I saw Ginger McColl. He was walking over from his post with P5. Walking. Holding on to the crazily twisted rails of the ship and laughing at me.

'You're a lucky lot of sods, you are. You're all right. That was our gun, that was. Lifted the whole ruddy gun right out.

9

Last I saw was that bloke Jarvis with it, looking as if he was holding the gun in his great mitt, like he holds a water-polo ball.'

Then I saw why he was walking oddly. His uniform was ragged, what was left of it. Just a torn shirt and part of his trousers. One leg was shot off, and there was the splintered bone, dripping red and black blood, and white strings of sinews. My throat was full of spittle, and I could vomit just to look at him. I thought the world of Ginger.

'I must go and get this wrapped up,' was all he said, then hobbled off guiding his way through the smoke and clutching the twisted rail.

'Let's get,' I said, and the rest of our lot followed me, clambering up towards the flight deck. In the grey steel plating was the shell hole. The first shell hole I'd ever seen. Fascinated, I gazed at the jagged edge. A young sailor came screaming down the ladder from the deck, and he was clutching the rails with both hands, kicking out with both feet. I could see he wasn't injured, only hysterical.

'Cut it out,' said Taff. 'Cut it out, lad.'

And he lunged out and hit the kid a welt across the face so hard it sent him staggering back against the deck. The kid stopped screaming all right.

We ran on. There was the hangar, the wall of fire still rising.

... There was nothing we could do here. But the lower hangar? Half a dozen of us ran to the nearest watertight door, which by wartime routine was always closed. One man alone couldn't undo the great lock. So we all clambered for a handhold.

Another swing and we've done it, boys. ... With our combined weight we heaved, and the door gave. It gave so suddenly we were all flung on our backsides, and the flame gushed out like the very flames of hell. I thought the huge steel door of the hangar would never swing back. It was like the boiler end of an express train coming up at you.

We scrambled up, cursing the fire, cursing the door,

shouting to one another for help to get it shut again, as the giant inrush of air gave new zest to the furnace. As tongues of flame shot out, I got to one side of the door with Taff, and as we began to heave it shut there was a sight on the deck such as I could never picture even in a nightmare.

The wheel lock of that door had huge starfish spokes. The spokes of that wheel had pinned one of the crew, running right through his body with a clear X pattern like a bruised hot-cross bun. He must have died instantly, the way the imprint of the wheel was left right through his diaphragm. And there was a bit of his shirt, squelching blood, still hanging from the wheel lock.

I reckon we went berserk at that door. But somehow we got it shut, imprisoned the flames that by now were eating the heart out of *Glorious*. We dripped sweat with the effort and were blackened by the flames. But I still had my jacket on. That was damn silly. So I took it off, and laid it over the punctured corpse on the deck.

By now the *Glorious* was listing, and all the filth was draining that way across the slanting decks.

... Just then we got the order to abandon ship and, kicking our way through the stacks of empty shell-cases which we hadn't time to fling over after the live projjies, we marched off, quite orderly, to our special stations.

And then we marched back.

The abandon ship order was cancelled almost as soon as we got it, and we got the action stations again.

... The abandon ship order came again soon after – not in the precise metallic way of the Tannoy but with one of the officers running along the battery shouting words which on the *Glorious* sounded brutally unreal. 'Abandon ship. . . . All hands prepare to abandon ship. . . .'

And off we went like sheep, a thin file of bewildered, scorched and oil-scarred men, joining the throngs of others struggling against the sharply listing deck until we became a flood of humanity, pressing through the shell debris and the wreckage, running with the ugly current of a crowd towards our appointed stations for abandon ship.

We knew where to go. Week after week, in peacetime and in war, we'd practised it. A lot of bull, just to conform to regulations. We'd never need to know....

Week after week we went through the motions, but not through the actions. That's the part of the deck you'll stand on, but for Christ's sake don't stand on it now when I've just swabbed it down. That's the guy-rope you'll hang on, but don't hang on the blamed thing now, because it's just been painted.

Now the decks were deep in dust and debris, and the new paint scorched as we were ourselves, and we stood there in flocks, sheep-like, wondering what came next after the order abandon ship. We'd never been told what came next.

One or two of the lads took the order literally and threw themselves over the rails.

'For God's sake, come back!' their pals screamed after them as they dived off the listing deck; but it was no use. The speed we'd been travelling when the action was at its height meant the *Glorious* still had way on her, and to dive into that white frothing cauldron now meant being left miles behind without a hope of rescue.

We felt perplexed because up to this awful moment we'd been obeying orders, and now there weren't any more orders to obey. What comes after abandon ship?...

Then it was we saw how wonderful the officers could be. There were the hordes of bruised and injured men waiting like an untidy crowd at the end of a seaside pier, and there was the major of marines and two other officers by the hatchway leading down from the centre of the quarterdeck.

'Come on, lads. Don't panic now. Get into line....'

It was nothing they said, really. But the way they stood there and said it. They could have buggered off and left us.

Orders were what we wanted, so they gave us orders. 'You and you and you. That's right, lads. The three of you. Check the cutter in the storage bay....'

We checked it.

In the next bay to where I was standing was storage for a motor-driven cutter, a thirty-foot clinker-built job. Now the planking was shelled and jagged. The transom was split off. The launching cradle was smashed. And anyway we could not launch the thing because of the list of the ship. But we checked it, like we'd been told to do.

There were useful, purposeful things to do as well. There was the job of getting floatable things off that were undamaged. There was the idea of getting some rations in case any of the ship's boats had no fresh stores or water; but this was now too late and impossible. There was the matter of tending to the men who had not been injured seriously enough during the action to be taken to the first-aid posts, but who were now flagging from the strain and shock.

Next to me was a matelot suffering from gunshock, and he kept on trying to vomit until his frame was weak with retching. Somewhere in my trousers pocket I found the sticky paper of glucose sweets, and he sucked them and gave me a bit of a smile. That stopped it.

By now the quarterdeck was sloping at an angle of nearly forty-five degrees and, as each man prepared to jump, it meant a struggle to climb up for it. Little knots of men clawed each other round the waist as they clambered up the rails, laughing and swearing as they stripped off their boots and trousers and prepared to jump.

Then my turn came. I got to the top of the deck, and stood there looking down. It must have been thirty feet. And down there I saw the ship's screw on the starboard side still churning beneath me.

It was going to be one hell of a jump. I didn't want to hit that ruddy great green bronze screw, nor any of those oily black bobbing heads in the water.

'Teach you to drown, young 'un!'

A voice was driving through my brain. It was my brother Bill. We were at New Brighton again, when I was a kid and he was teaching me to swim. Swim? Well, he held me up by the chin, then yelled: 'Teach you to drown, young 'un,' and he let me go. A couple of mouthfuls, I kicked out. And I could swim. No foot on the bottom. I could really swim.

'*Teach you to drown, young 'un.* . . .'

That laughing voice followed me as I jumped.

3   Save Our Souls

Elspeth Huxley

Being shipwrecked is a horrible enough event in anyone's life. But for many who were not immediately rescued the aftermath was even worse. For days, even weeks sometimes, these unfortunate sailors found themselves clinging to bits of flotsam or swilling about in a lifeboat, covered in oil, freezing, weak from hunger and thirst. It was a living hell from which thousands never returned.

On 17 September 1940 the merchantman *City of Benares*, carrying ninety children among its passengers from Britain to safety in Canada, was torpedoed and sunk. On one lifeboat that escaped the wreck were thirty-two East Indians from the crew, six small boys, a Miss Mary Cornish, who had been helping to look after the children, and the fourth officer, who took charge of the lifeboat. Elspeth Huxley described their fate after the sinking of their ship. It was a fate typical of that endured by a great many people during the days of the war.

They had been a week at sea.

The strength of the boys was ebbing fast. They had barely eaten for five days; and their thirst was becoming acute. Almost as bad was the constant pressure against other bodies, the aching of bruised muscles, and the pain of sleepless bloodshot eyes. Several of the East Indians were lying semi-conscious in the bottom of the boat. Still the lifeboat kept her course, under sail now, for the sea was a little calmer.

At noon the steward brought round the usual water ration, which each person poured into his empty condensed milk tin. This was the last time – although the steward did not tell them then – that they would get water at noon. Next day the ration was to be halved, and water issued only in the evening. They were nearing the bottom of the cask.

The delirious boy recovered with the coming of daylight, although he was weak, and his feet were sore. Thirsty or not, that evening the boys still wanted their bedtime instalment of Captain Drummond, and Mary Cornish gave it to them. She found the effort considerable, for not only was it difficult to speak with a parched, dry throat and a swollen tongue, but a week with little food and water, and with constant anxiety over the boys, had begun to affect her mind. She had to force her thoughts with conscious effort, like squeezing hardened paint out of a tube. But she managed to think of the day's plot somehow, although her voice sounded thick and barely intelligible in her own ears.

That evening messages came down from the stern that the East Indians were restive and needed to be watched. On board was a hatchet used to split open cases of canned provisions. This was kept in the bows, and the escorts, by way of precaution, put it down within easy reach.

After nightfall another of the boys became delirious. His feet were so painful that he could not bear to have them touched. As the night wore on he became obsessed with the fear of going mad. By some trick of the moonlight, shadows from the rigging were falling across him in dark bars. To his delirious mind these seemed to him to be the real bars of a prison, and he shouted to be let out, rolling from side to side in fear. Sometimes he screamed horribly, and shouted, 'I'm mad, I'm going mad, I *know* I'm going mad.'

A message came down from the stern: could the escorts for God's sake keep that boy quiet, his screams might drive the East Indians over the edge. Mary Cornish tried to calm him, but if anyone touched him he shouted all the more. Father O'Sullivan said in French: 'This boy is dying of thirst.'

A message went back to the steward: could he spare an extra dipperful of water? A few drops were smuggled past the East Indians by one of the seamen coming off duty. But after this no more could be done. Only one torch with a live battery was left on board, and the East Indians had it. They were keeping its beam trained on the sick boy in the bows. They were not taking any chances; no one was going to cheat them of their share of water by giving an extra ration to the sick boy.

There was one service that the priest alone could perform. He took the boy in his arms and offered prayers for his soul. The others could not understand the rapid Latin phrases, but the boys trusted him, and his low-voiced words had a soothing effect.

There was a disturbance among the East Indians, and then the gunner appeared. He took in the situation at a glance: the kneeling priest, the prayers for the dying, and the solemn atmosphere.

'What's going on here *now*?' he demanded. 'What's wrong with the poor little blighter?'

The boy, croaking like a frog, cried out for water.

'Water?' the gunner said. 'Is *that* all? Of course you want water; we all do. You'll get your water in the morning.'

The boy only cried out again for a drink.

'Now you forget about it,' the gunner commanded. 'You'll have plenty of water when we're picked up, and that won't be long now. Is *that* all that's wrong with you?'

'My feet are cold,' the boy answered weakly.

The gunner snorted triumphantly, and glared at the escorts. 'Huh! So your feet are cold. That's a nice way to look after a kid....'

He rearranged Mary Cornish's jacket round the boy's legs. 'Are your feet warm *now*?'

The boy mumbled: 'My feet are cold.'

The cadet, who was off duty in the bows, took off his overcoat, and the gunner wrapped this also round the sick boy's feet.

'There. Any better?' he demanded.

'My feet are cold.'

'No, they're not,' the gunner said firmly. 'They're

wrapped up properly now, and they'll be as warm as toast in half a jiffy. Now – are your feet warm?'

'My feet . . .' the boy began.

'Don't let me hear another sound out of you till the morning,' the gunner said fiercely. 'No more of this yelling out. Now – *are your feet warm?*'

'Yes,' the boy whispered feebly.

'Then you'll be all right till the morning.'

He went off, muttering under his breath about boys with cold feet, women who didn't know how to look after kids, and the respective merits of saying prayers and keeping children warm. His methods were effective; the atmosphere was changed. The boy did not scream any more, and when his companion, who had been delirious the night before, offered to lie down beside him, he gradually quietened down.

. . . It was a boy who first saw the flying-boat. With a cry of 'Sunderland', he pointed to the west. A speck in the sky was growing larger. Nobody believed it at first. A dozen Sunderlands had already been sighted, only to resolve themselves into gulls. But this time it was real. By a freak of chance the path of a flying-boat patrolling far out into the Atlantic had crossed their own.

4 Contact... contact

Donald MacIntyre

Submarines came into their own during the Second World War. German U-boats almost succeeded in completely crippling Britain's vitally important merchant navy. Allied undersea fleets played a crucial part in achieving final victory, a part out of all proportion to their comparatively small numbers of men and ships.

Britain's first problem in the early months of the battle was to cope with the German U-boats raiding in the Atlantic. Convoys, so successfully used in the First World War, were the solution. Merchant ships were not allowed to sail independently but were gathered into small fleets which were escorted across the ocean by two or three Royal Navy warships – destroyers, frigates or corvettes, mostly.

Even then, however, losses were heavy. The U-boats worked in pairs or in larger formations, called wolfpacks, attacking a convoy from many directions at the same time, thus making it almost impossible for the escort vessels to protect the convoy effectively.

Two of the most successful U-boat commanders were Otto Kretschmer in U-99 and Joachim Schepke in U-100. Each sank at least 250 000 tonnes of Allied shipping. Strangely enough, both U-boats were sunk on the same day, their commanders' careers ended at last. They were attacking Convoy HX112 on 17 March 1941, as Captain Donald MacIntyre DSO and two bars, DSC, RN, described in his book *U-Boat Killer*. MacIntyre was in command of the senior escort vessel that day, HMS *Walker*. With him was HMS *Vanoc*. The U-boats began by scoring heavily; but then their luck changed.

In the next hour five ships were torpedoed. I was near to despair and I racked my brains to find some way to stop the holocaust. While the convoy stayed in impeccable formation, we escorts raced about in the exasperating business of searching in vain for the almost invisible enemy. Our one hope was to sight a U-boat's telltale white wake, give chase to force her to dive, and so give the Asdics a chance to bring our depth charges into action. Everything had to be subordinated to that end and so, with binoculars firmly wedged on a steady bearing, I put *Walker* into a gently curving course, thereby putting every point of the compass under a penetrating probe. It worked.

As her bows swung, a thin line of white water came into the lens of my glasses, a thin line which could only be the wake of a ship. There were none of ours in that direction; it had to be a U-boat! I shouted orders increasing speed to thirty knots and altered course towards the target. Suddenly, the U-boat spotted us and in a cloud of spray he crash-dived. A swirl of phosphorescent water still lingered as we passed over the spot and sent a pattern of ten depth charges crashing down. We could hardly have missed; it had been so quick we must have dropped them smack on top of him. Then the depth charges exploded with great cracking explosions and giant water spouts rose to masthead height astern of us. Two and a half minutes later another explosion followed and an orange flash spread momentarily across the surface. We had every reason to hope that this was our first 'kill'.

Though we learned that this was not so, for our charges had exploded too deeply to do him fatal damage, we felt almost certain at the time when our Asdic search showed no trace of a contact. *Vanoc* came racing past to rejoin the convoy and offered assistance. I refused this, convinced as I was that we could safely leave the scene with a 'probable' marked down in the log-book, and ordered her back to her station.

However, no U-boat was officially recorded as destroyed without tangible evidence and I continued the Asdic search until such time as wreckage should come to the surface.

It was just as well. For half an hour later we gained contact with a certain U-boat. Our prey had not been 'killed'; he was, in fact, sneaking back towards the convoy, still bent on attack.

Recalling *Vanoc* to assist in the hunt, we set about our target with a series of carefully aimed patterns of depth charges.

Taking it in turns to run in to the attack, pattern after pattern of depth charges went down as we tried to get one to within the lethal range of about twenty feet of our target. But he was a wily opponent and, dodging and twisting in the depths, he managed to escape destruction though heavily damaged.

Soon the waters became so disturbed by the repeated explosions, each one of which sent back an echo to the Asdic's sound beam, that we could no longer distinguish our target from the other echoes and a lull in the fight was forced upon us.

I had for some time past noticed in the distance the bobbing lights from the lifeboats of one of our sunken ships, but with an enemy to engage there was nothing for it but to harden my heart and hope that the time might come later when I could rescue the crews. This lull seemed a good opportunity and perhaps if we left the area temporarily the U-boat commander might think he had shaken us off and be tempted into some indiscretion. So, the *Vanoc* steaming round us in protection, we stopped and picked up the master and thirty-seven of the crew of the SS *J. B. White*.

This completed, the time was ripe to head quietly back to where the U-boat had last been located and perhaps catch him licking his wounds on the surface.

We had hardly got under way when I noticed that *Vanoc* was drawing ahead fast and thought perhaps she had misread the signal ordering the speed to be maintained. As I ordered a signal to be made to her, Yeoman of Signals Gerrard said, 'She's signalling to us, sir, but I can't read it as her light is flickering so badly.' I realised that *Vanoc* must be going ahead at her full speed and being, like *Walker*, an old veteran, her bridge would be shaking and rattling as her

30 000 h.p. drove her forward through the Atlantic swell.

Rupert Bray, on the bridge beside me, said, 'She must have sighted the U-boat.' Even as he spoke, *Vanoc* came on the air with his radio telephone, with the laconic signal: 'Have rammed and sunk U-boat.'

What a blissful moment that was for us, the successful culmination of a long and arduous fight. Something in the way of revenge for our losses in the convoy had been achieved.

There was grim joy on board *Walker*, and not least amongst the merchant seamen from the *J. B. White*, who felt they had a personal score to settle. But for the moment our part was confined to circling *Vanoc* in protection, while she picked up the few survivors from the U-boat and examined herself for damage. We were glad of this breathing space, as, with all the depth charges carried on the upper deck expended, the depth-charge party, led by Leading Seaman Prout, were struggling to hoist up more of these awkward heavy loads from the magazine, with the ship rolling in the Atlantic swell, and often with water swirling round their waists. They were not a moment too soon, for, as we circled *Vanoc*, I was electrified to hear the Asdic operator Able Seaman Backhouse excitedly reporting, 'Contact, contact.' But I could hardly credit it, for not only was it unbelievable that in all the wide wastes of the Atlantic a second U-boat should turn up just where another had gone to the bottom, but I knew that there were sure to be areas of disturbed water persisting in the vicinity from our own and *Vanoc*'s wakes. The echo was not very clear and I expressed my doubts to John Langton, but Backhouse was not to be disheartened. 'Contact definitely submarine,' he reported, and as I listened to the ping, the echo sharpened and there could be no further doubt. With a warning to the men aft to get any charges ready that they had managed to hoist into the throwers and rails, we ran into the attack. It was a great test for John Langton, for, with the maddening habit of the beautiful instruments of precision provided for us, they all elected to break down at the crucial moment. But much patient drill against just such an emergency now brought its reward. Timing his attack by the most primitive methods Langton gave the order to fire. A pattern of six depth charges – all that could be got ready in time – went down. As they exploded, *Walker* ran on to get sea-room to turn for further attacks, but as we turned came the thrilling signal from *Vanoc* – 'U-boat surfaced astern of me.'

A searchlight beam stabbed into the night from *Vanoc*, illuminating the submarine U-99, which lay stopped. The guns' crews in both ships sprang into action and the blinding flashes from the four-inch guns and tracers from the smaller weapons made a great display, though I fear their accuracy was not remarkable. Destroyer night gunnery in such a mêlée is apt to be pretty wild and in those days, when flashless cordite was not issued to us, each salvo left one temporarily blinded. In *Walker* confusion soon reigned around the guns, for the enthusiasm of our guests from *J. B. White* knew no bounds. Joining up with the ammunition supply parties, shells came up at such a phenomenal rate that the decks were piled high with them till the guns' crews were hardly able to work their guns. But fortunately we were able very soon to cease fire as a signal lamp flashing from the U-boat, 'We are sunking' [*sic*], made it clear that the action was over. Keeping end-on to the U-boat in case he still had some fight left, we prepared to lower a boat in case there was a chance of a capture, but even as we did so the crew of the U-boat abandoned ship and she plunged to the bottom.

I manoeuvred *Walker* to windward of the swimming Germans and as we drifted down on to them, they were hauled on board. Some of them were in the last stages of exhaustion from the cold of those icy northern waters by the time we got them on board. Some indeed would never have made safety had not Leading Seaman Prout gone over the side fully clothed to aid them.

The last to come over the side was obviously the captain,

as he swam to *Walker* still wearing his brass-bound cap. We were soon to find out that we had made indeed a notable capture, for the captain was Otto Kretschmer, leading ace of the U-boat arm, holder of the Knight's Cross with oak leaves and top scorer in terms of tonnage sunk.

5 The end of an era

O'Dowd Gallagher

For over two hundred years the Royal Navy was master of the seas. Hitler's warships challenged that supremacy but never overcame the British fleet. It was the Japanese who brought the end of the era of British naval invincibility.

On Sunday, 7 December 1941 Japan attacked suddenly, and without warning, the United States base, Pearl Harbor, thus entering the war and dragging America with her. On 10 December the Japanese attacked the British Far East Fleet.

O'Dowd Gallagher was a war correspondent aboard HMS *Repulse*; he reported the engagement for his newspaper, *The Daily Express*, which published the account on 12 December 1941. The British navy never recovered from its defeat that day; from then on the American navy took over in the Pacific.

At 11 a.m. a twin-masted single-funnel ship is sighted on the starboard bow. The force goes to investigate her. She carries no flag.

I was looking at her through my telescope when the shock of an explosion made me jump so that I nearly poked my right eye out. It was 11.15 a.m. The explosion came from the *Prince of Wales*'s port-side secondary armament. She was firing at a single aircraft.

We open fire. There are about six aircraft.

A three-quarter-inch screw falls on my tin hat from the bridge deck above from the shock of explosion of the guns. 'The old tub's falling to bits,' observes the yeoman of signals.

That was the beginning of a superb air attack by the Japanese, whose air force was an unknown quantity.

Officers in the *Prince of Wales* whom I met in their wardroom when she arrived here last week said they expected

25

some unorthodox flying from the Japanese. 'The great danger will be the possibility of these chaps flying their whole aircraft into a ship and committing hara-kiri.'

It was nothing like that. It was most orthodox. They even came at us in formation, flying low and close.

Aboard the *Repulse* I found observers as qualified as anyone to estimate Japanese flying abilities. They know from first-hand experience what the RAF and the Luftwaffe are like. Their verdict was: 'The Germans have never done anything like this in the North Sea, Atlantic or anywhere else we have been.'

They concentrated on the two capital ships, taking the *Prince of Wales* first and the *Repulse* second. The destroyer screen they left completely alone except for damaged planes forced to fly low over them when they dropped bombs defensively.

At 11.18 the *Prince of Wales* opened a shattering barrage with all her multiple pompoms or 'Chicago pianos' as they call them. Red and blue flames poured from the eight-gun muzzles of each battery.

I saw glowing tracer shells describe shallow curves as they went soaring skyward surrounding the enemy planes. Our 'Chicago pianos' opened fire; also our triple-gun four-inch high-angle turrets. The uproar was so tremendous I seemed to feel it.

From the starboard side of the flag deck I can see two torpedo planes. No, they're bombers. Flying straight at us.

All our guns pour high explosives at them, including shells so delicately fused that they explode if they merely graze cloth fabric.

But they swing away, carrying out a high-powered evasive action without dropping anything at all. I realise now what the purpose of the action was. It was a diversion to occupy all our guns and observers on the air-defence platform at the summit of the mainmast.

There is a heavy explosion and the *Repulse* rocks. Great patches of paint fall from the funnel on to the flag deck. We all gaze above our heads to see planes which during the action against the low fliers were unnoticed.

They are high-level bombers. Seventeen thousand feet. The first bomb, the one that rocked us a moment ago, scored a direct hit on the catapult deck through the one hangar on the port side.

I am standing behind a multiple Vickers gun, one which fires 2000 half-inch bullets per minute. It is at the after-end of the flag deck.

I see a cloud of smoke rising from the place where the first bomb hit. Another comes down bang again from 17 000 feet. It explodes in the sea, making a creamy blue-and-green patch ten feet across. The *Repulse* rocks again. It was three fathoms from the port side. It was a miss, so no one bothers.

Cooling fluid is spurting from one of the barrels of a 'Chicago piano'. I can see black paint on the funnel-shaped covers at the muzzles of eight barrels actually rising in blisters big as fists.

The boys manning them – there are ten to each – are sweating, saturating their asbestos anti-flash helmets. The whole gun swings this way and that as spotters pick planes to be fired at.

Two planes can be seen coming at us. A spotter sees another at a different angle, but much closer.

He leans forward, his face tight with excitement, urgently pounding the back of the gun swiveller in front of him. He hits that back with his right hand and points with the left a stabbing forefinger at a single sneaker plane. Still blazing two-pounders, the whole gun platform turns in a hail of death at the single plane. It is some 1000 yards away.

I saw tracers rip into its fuselage dead in the centre. Its fabric opened up like a rapidly spreading sore with red edges. Fire. . . .

It swept to the tail, and in a moment stabiliser and rudder became a framework skeleton. Her nose dipped down and she went waterward.

We cheered like madmen. I felt the larynx tearing in the

effort to make myself heard above the hellish uproar of guns.

A plane smacked the sea on its belly and was immediately transformed into a gigantic shapeless mass of fire which shot over the waves fast as a snake's tongue. The *Repulse* had got the first raider.

For the first time since the action began we can hear a sound from the loudspeakers, which are on every deck at every action station. It is the sound of a bugle.

Its first notes are somewhat tortured. The young bugler's lips and throat are obviously dry with excitement. It is that most sinister alarm of all for seamen: 'Fire!'

Smoke from our catapult deck is thick now. Men in overalls, their faces hidden by a coat of soot, manhandle hoses along decks. Water fountains delicately from a rough patch made in one section by binding it with a white shirt.

It sprays on the Vickers gunners, who, in a momentary lull, lift faces, open mouths and put out tongues to catch the cool-looking jets. They quickly avert faces to spit – the water is salt and it is warm. It is sea water.

The 'Chicago pianos' open up again with a suddenness that I am unable to refrain from flinching at, though once they get going with their erratic shell-pumping it is most reassuring.

All aboard have said the safest place in any battleship or cruiser or destroyer is behind a 'Chicago piano'. I believe them.

Empty brass cordite cases are tumbling out of the gun's scuttle-like exit so fast and so excitedly it reminds me of the forbidden fruit machine in Gibraltar on which I once played. It went amok on one occasion and ejected eight pounds in shillings in a frantic rush.

The cases bounce off the steel C deck, roll and dance down the sloping base into a channel for easy picking up later.

At 11.25 we see an enormous splash on the very edge of the horizon. The splash vanishes and a whitish cloud takes its place.

A damaged enemy plane jettisoning its bombs or another enemy destroyed? A rapid Gallup poll on the flag deck says: 'Another duck down.' Duck is a word they have rapidly taken from the Aussie navy. It means enemy plane.

Hopping about the flag deck from port to starboard, whichever side is being attacked, is the plump figure of a naval photographer named Tubby Abrahams.

He was a Fleet Street agency pictureman, now in the Navy. But all his pictures are lost. He had to throw them into the sea with his camera. He was saved. So was United States broadcaster Cecil Brown, of Columbia Broadcasting System.

Fire parties are still fighting the hangar outbreak, oblivious of any air attacks so far. Bomb splinters have torn three holes in the starboard side of the funnel on our flag deck.

Gazing impotently with no more than fountain pen and notebook in my hands while gunners, signallers, surgeons, and rangefinders worked, I found emotional release in shouting rather stupidly, I suppose, at the Japanese.

I discovered depths of obscenity previously unknown, even to me.

One young signaller keeps passing me pieces of information in between running up flags. He has just said: 'A couple of blokes are caught in the lift from galley to servery. They're trying to get them out.'

The yeoman of signals interjected: 'How the bloody hell they got there, God knows.'

There is a short lull. The boys dig inside their overalls and pull out cigarettes. Then the loudspeaker voice: 'Enemy aircraft ahead.' Lighted ends are nipped off cigarettes. The ship's company goes into action again. 'Twelve of them.' The flag-deck boys whistle. Someone counts them aloud: 'One, two, three, four, five, six, seven, eight, nine – yes, nine.' The flag-deck wag, as he levels a signalling lamp at the *Prince of Wales*: 'Any advance on nine? Anybody? No? Well here they come.'

It is 12.10 p.m. They are all concentrating on the *Prince of Wales*. They are after the big ships, all right. A mass of water and smoke rises in a tree-like column from the *Prince of Wales*'s stern. They've got her with a torpedo.

A ragged-edge mass of flame from her 'Chicago piano' does not stop them, nor the heavy instant flashes from her high-angle secondary armament.

She is listing to port – a bad list. We are about six cables from her.

A snottie, or midshipman, runs past, calls as he goes: '*Prince of Wales*'s steering gear gone.' It doesn't seem possible that those slight-looking planes could do that to her.

The planes leave us, having apparently dropped all their bombs and torpedoes. I don't believe it is over, though. 'Look, look!' shouts someone, 'there's a line in the water right under our bows, growing longer on the starboard side. A torpedo that missed us. Wonder where it'll stop.'

The *Prince of Wales* signals us again, asking if we've been torpedoed. Our Captain Tennant replies: 'Not yet. We've dodged nineteen.'

Six stokers arrive on the flag deck. They are black with smoke and oil and in need of first aid. They are ushered down to the armoured citadel at the base of the mainmast.

The *Prince of Wales*'s list is increasing. There is a great rattle of empty two-pounder cordite cases as 'Chicago piano' boys gather up the empties to stow them away and clear for further action.

12.20 p.m. . . . The end is near, although I didn't know it.

A new wave of planes appears, flying around us in formation and gradually coming nearer. The *Prince of Wales* lies about ten cables astern of our port side. She is helpless.

They are making for her. I don't know how many. They are splitting up our guns as we realise they are after her, knowing she can't dodge their torpedoes. So we fire at them to defend the *Prince of Wales* rather than attend to our own safety.

The only analogy I can think of to give an impression of

the *Prince of Wales* in those last moments is of a mortally wounded tiger trying to beat off the *coup de grâce*.

Her outuine is hardly distinguishable in smoke and flame from all her guns except the fourteen-inchers. I can see one plane release a torpedo. It drops nose-heavy into the sea and churns up a small wake as it drives straight at the *Prince of Wales*. It explodes against her bows.

A couple of seconds later another explodes amidships and another astern. Gazing at her turning over on the port side with her stern going under and with dots of men leaping from her, I am thrown against the bulkhead by a tremendous shock as the *Repulse* takes a torpedo on her port-side astern.

With all others on the flag deck I am wondering where it came from when the *Repulse* shudders gigantically. Another torpedo.

Now men cheering with more abandon than at a Cup Final. What the heck is this? I wonder. Then see it is another plane down. It hits the sea in flames also. There have been six, so far as I know.

My notebook, which I have got before me, is stained with oil and is ink-blurred. It says: 'Third torp.'

The *Repulse* now listing badly to starboard. The loud-speakers speak for the last time: 'Everybody on main deck.'

We all troop down ladders, most orderly except for one lad who climbs the rail and is about to jump when an officer says: 'Now then – come back – we are all going your way.' The boy came back and joined the line.

It seemed slow going. Like all the others, I suppose I was tempted to leap to the lower deck, but the calmness was catching. When we got to the main deck the list was so bad our shoed feet could not grip the steel deck. I kicked off mine, and my damp stockinged feet made for sure movement.

Nervously opening my cigarette case, I found I hadn't a match. I offered a cigarette to a man beside me. He said: 'Ta. Want a match?' We both lit up and puffed once or twice. He said: 'We'll be seeing you, mate.' To which I replied: 'Hope so. Cheerio.'

We were all able to walk down the ship's starboard side, she lay so much over to port.

We all formed a line along a big protruding anti-torpedo blister, from where we had to jump some twelve feet into a sea which was black – I discovered it was oil.

I remember jamming my cap on my head, drawing a breath and leaping.

Oh, I forgot – the last entry in my notebook was: 'Sank about 12.20 p.m.' I made it before leaving the flag deck. In the water I glimpsed the *Prince of Wales*'s bows disappearing.

Kicking with all my strength, I with hundreds of others tried to get away from the *Repulse* before she went under, being afraid of getting drawn under in the whirlpool.

I went in the wrong direction, straight into the still spreading oil patch, which felt almost as thick as velvet. A wave hit me and swung me round so that I saw the last of the *Repulse*.

Her underwater plates were painted a bright, light red. Her bows rose high as the air trapped inside tried to escape from underwater forward regions, and there she hung for a second or two and easily slid out of sight.

I had a tremendous feeling of loneliness, and could see nothing capable of carrying me. I kicked, lying on my back, and felt my eyes burning as the oil crept over me, in mouth, nostrils and hair.

When swamped by the waves I remember seeing the water I spurted from my mouth was black. I came across two men hanging on to a round lifebelt. They were black, and I told them they looked like a couple of Al Jolsons. They said: 'Well, we must be a trio, 'cos you're the same.'

We were joined by another, so we had an Al Jolson quartet on one lifebelt. It was too much for it, and in the struggle to keep it lying flat on the sea we lost it.

We broke up, with the possibility of meeting again, but

none of us would know the other, owing to the complete mask of oil.

I kicked, I must confess somewhat panicky, to escape from the oil, but all I achieved was a bumping into a floating paravane. Once again there were four black faces with red eyes gathered together in the sea.

Then we saw a small motorboat with two men in it. The engine was broken. I tried to organise our individual strengths into a concerted drive to reach the idly floating boat. We tried to push or pull ourselves by hanging on the paravane, kicking our legs, but it was too awkward, and it overturned.

I lost my grip and went under. My underwater struggles happily took me nearer to the boat.

After about two hours in the water, two hours of oil-fuel poisoning, I reached a thin wire rope which hung from the boat's bows.

My fingers were numb, and I was generally weak as the result of the poisoning, but I managed to hold on to the wire by clamping my arms around it. I called to the men aboard to help me climb the four feet to the deck.

They tried with a boat-hook, but finally said: 'You know, we are pretty done in, too. You've got to try to help yourself. We can't do it alone.'

I said I could not hold anything. They put the boat-hook in my shirt collar, but it tore, and finally they said: 'Sorry, pal, we can't lift you. Have you got that wire?'

'Yes,' I said. They let me go, and there I hung. Another man arrived and caught the wire. He was smaller than I was. I am thirteen stone. The men aboard said they would try to get him up. 'He's lighter than you,' they said.

They got him aboard, during which operation I went under again when he put his foot on my shoulder. The mouth of one black face aboard opened and showed black-slimed teeth, red gums and tongue. It said: 'To hell with this.'

He dived through the oil into the sea, popped up beside

me with a round lifebelt, which he put over my head, saying: 'OK. Now let go the wire.'

But I'm sorry to say I couldn't. I couldn't bear to part with it. It had kept me on the surface about fifteen minutes.

They separated us, however, and the next thing I was draped through the lifebelt like a dummy being hauled aboard at a rope's end, which they could grip as it was not oily or slimy.

Another oil casualty was dragged aboard, and later thirty of us were lifted aboard a destroyer. We were stripped, bathed and left naked on the fo'c'sle benches and tables to sweat the oil out of the pores in the great heat.

Admiral Sir Tom Phillips was last seen close beside Captain Leach. They were in the armoured bridge, and were seen slipping as the *Prince of Wales* heeled over, and the bridge got to water level.

So it is probable that Britain loses yet another brilliant naval officer, because of the time-honoured tradition that captains must be the last to leave their ships.

Captain William Tennant, of *Repulse*, and his commander leaped at the last minute into the sea together, with a senior petty officer, both officers being dressed in long white trousers and tunics. Tennant's head hit a piece of floating wood, but he managed to keep swimming till rescued.

A remarkable feature of the Japanese attack is that their bombers did not have any fighter escort. Once the *Prince of Wales* and the *Repulse* sank, the planes left without bothering the destroyers.

6 The sauciest job since Drake

Donald MacIntyre

1942 was a grim year. The war settled into a seemingly everlasting nightmare. At sea the U-boats fought hard and killed often. But the Allies began to hit back, not only against the submarines but also by mounting seaborne operations against carefully selected enemy targets.

One such was the raid on the German-occupied port of St Nazaire. Donald MacIntyre explains the reason for the operation and describes the action in this chapter extracted from his book *Fighting Ships and Fighting Seamen*.

At 2 p.m. on 26 March 1942 a flotilla of little ships sailed unobtrusively from Falmouth harbour. It comprised sixteen motor launches (ML) one motor torpedo boat (MTB) and one motor gunboat (MGB). Following them out of harbour came three destroyers, two of which, *Atherstone* and *Tynedale*, belonged to the modern, up-to-date class of small escort destroyers of the 'Hunt' class; the third, though wearing the White Ensign of the Royal Navy and the name *Campbeltown*, had originally been built many years before for the United States Navy, one of the numerous class known as 'Four-Stackers' which had been made over to Great Britain in 1940 in return for the lease to America of certain bases on British territory. The *Campbeltown*'s silhouette had been considerably altered since then, her four slender funnels having been replaced by two stubbier ones, so that she now looked vaguely German.

On reaching the open Channel, the force turned south-westward and headed out into the Atlantic. Operation 'Chariot' was under way. In the greatest secrecy had been

35

prepared what Colonel Newman, the officer in command of the troops embarked in the ships, called the 'sauciest job since Drake' – nothing less than the destruction of the biggest dry dock in the world at St Nazaire in German-occupied France, some miles up the heavily defended estuary of the Loire. The dock was the only one outside Germany available to the enemy which could take the huge battleship *Tirpitz*.

Its destruction would mean that the battleship would almost certainly not venture out into the Atlantic, which would relieve the Admiralty of one of its most pressing anxieties and release for other urgent duties the large naval force which had otherwise to be held ready to deal with such a contingency. The risks involved in such an operation were enormous. Casualties were bound to be high. But it was hoped that a combination of surprise and a diversionary air raid would reduce them as well as ensure success.

The main item in the operation was to be the ramming of the outer lock-gates – or more properly, 'caisson', pronounced cassoon – of the dry dock by a ship loaded with explosives with a delay-action fuse. Demolition squads were to blow up the inner caisson, the pumping station and the caisson winding mechanism as well as to be prepared to destroy the outer caisson if anything went wrong with the ramming operation.

The role of explosive ship had been given to the veteran *Campbeltown*, commanded by Lieutenant-Commander S. H. Beattie. Like some of her sisters, the *Campbeltown* had not proved too successful as a destroyer. She was now to be given the opportunity to atone in death for her shortcomings in life. The 91 officers and men of the demolition squads and the 166 fighting troops to escort and protect them while carrying out their tasks had been selected from army Commando formations. All were volunteers. Few had any strong belief in their chance of a safe return from the raid.

To put the troops ashore and, it was hoped, to bring them away again, were the sixteen MLs, 112-foot boats powered by two 650-horsepower petrol engines which gave them a maximum speed of eighteen knots. Their highly inflammable fuel, and wooden construction, made them so vulnerable as to be quite unsuited for a gun battle. Their proper function was hunting submarines so that their weapons consisted of torpedoes, depth charges and Lewis guns and a single three-pounder gun of Boer War date. Twelve of them now had their torpedoes removed and were fitted with two 20-millimetre Oerlikons in place of the three-pounder. The single MTB of the flotilla was armed with two engineless torpedoes, packed with 2200 lb of explosive and a delay-action fuse. These were intended to be fired at very close range and sunk to the bottom where they would explode underneath their target. It had seemed doubtful whether a suitable target for such weapons was likely to offer itself at St Nazaire, but the captain of MTB 74, Sub-Lieutenant R. C. M. V. Wynn, had pleaded to be included and it was decided that, in case the outer caisson was found to be open, he should take his craft into the dock and 'torpedo' the inner caisson. Alternatively he might be able to get through another entrance into the inner harbour and launch his weapons at the U-boat pens situated there. MTB 74 was an awkward bedmate, however. Her engines were highly temperamental, she could proceed at only two speeds – six knots or thirty-three – and her fuel endurance was so small that she had to make the passage to the Loire in tow of the *Campbeltown*.

Another craft which had to make the passage in tow was MGB 314, whose role was to act as headquarters ship for the joint commanders of the operation – Commander R. E. D. Ryder and Lieutenant-Colonel A. C. Newman – and their staffs. She was capable of twenty-six knots and was comparatively well-armed, having a two-pounder pompom, a two-pounder Rolls semi-automatic gun and two twin half-inch machine-guns.

Finally there were the two Hunt-class destroyers *Atherstone* and *Tynedale* which were to act as escort for the raiding craft. Ryder and Newman had embarked in the former and would transfer to the MGB in time to lead the raiding craft to their objective.

Such was the force which around midnight on 26 March passed far to seaward of Ushant, heading south into the Bay of Biscay. Let us look now at the enemy they were to meet. In and around St Nazaire and along the shore of the estuary were stationed some 6000 naval troops, manning coast defence guns – twenty-eight guns varying in calibre from 75 to 170 mm and a battery of 9.5-inch guns on railway mountings – and more than forty dual-purpose 'flak' guns of 40, 37 and 20 mm mounted on rooftops, on flak towers or on the tops of concrete bunkers. In addition there were four harbour defence boats, ten minesweepers and three armed tankers in all of which automatic weapons and machine-guns were mounted. Finally, lying in the river, in the path of any ships approaching the port, was a large auxiliary craft which mounted an 88-mm gun and several 20-mm Oerlikons.

It was, indeed, a veritable hornet's nest that would be aroused the moment an alarm was given. It was hoped, officially, that the defences would be so engrossed by the air raid which had been promised by Bomber Command of the RAF that they would not realise until late what was going on at ground level. But few amongst the gallant company of seamen and soldiers on their way to St Nazaire had any illusions as to what was in store for them.

By dawn on the 27th, the expedition had reached the position in the middle of the Bay of Biscay at which it was to turn eastwards and head for the French coast. Course had not long been altered when, from the bridge of the *Tynedale*, something that looked very like a surfaced submarine was sighted, some seven or eight miles on the port beam. Ordered by Ryder to investigate, the *Tynedale*, by means of German colours and a garbled reply to the U-boat's recognition signal, got to within 5000 yards before opening fire. Even this was too great a range to ensure a hit before the U-boat dived, however. Though the destroyer's first depth charge attack caused the submarine to break surface to be greeted with more gunfire before submerging again, a subsequent inconclusive hunt left Ryder with the possibility that the U-boat had survived. She would then be in a position to betray to the enemy the presence and, more important, the easterly course of his flotilla. He hoped, however, that at so great a distance the U-boat captain would have been unable to see the low-lying MLs. In this he was wrong, but luck was with him at this stage. U593, the submarine concerned, remained submerged for five and a half hours and then surfaced to report 'three destroyers and ten MTBs' – but gave their course as west! This mistake by the U-boat captain was doubly fortunate. Assuming that Ryder's force had been retiring after laying mines in the U-boat approach channels, the German Command ordered a flotilla of five destroyer-minesweepers to sea to carry out a mine reconnaissance. Thus these powerfully armed warships were absent from the port at the time of the raid.

Meanwhile the raiding force moved steadily eastwards, undetected. Soon after dark on the 27th it stopped to allow the commanders and their staff to tranship into the MGB which was then cast off from the parent destroyer, as was the MTB. With the MGB now leading, the flotilla set off again, the MLs in two columns with the *Campbeltown* between the second launch of each column, heading for a rendezvous with the submarine *Sturgeon* which had been stationed to seaward of the estuary as a marker beacon. At 10 p.m. her flashing signal winked out of the darkness exactly as planned. The *Campbeltown* and the MLs filed past her to the shouted good wishes of the submarine crew and now the *Atherstone* and *Tynedale* parted company. The raiders were on their own with only forty miles to go.

At a steady twelve knots they moved through the darkness, tension gradually growing, to silence the light-hearted badinage and wisecracking amongst the waiting Commandos. At 11 p.m. the time fuses of the *Campbeltown*'s explosive were activated to detonate at 7 a.m. At 11.30 the throb of aircraft engines announced the arrival of the bombers as scheduled; at the same time it began to rain. This thicker weather was welcomed by Ryder, but it was to have an unfortunate consequence in reducing the volume of the air raid and bringing it to a premature end. For the airmen had been restricted to bombing, from above 6000 feet, only the exact targets specified, which they had to identify clearly. Low cloud and rain would thus prevent them attacking. Half an hour after midnight, just as the naval force was entering the estuary of the Loire, the air raid died away.

Ashore, the German naval Captain Mecke, in command of the anti-aircraft brigade, had already been puzzled by the half-hearted efforts made by what was evidently a large force of aircraft. He had suspected at first that they were a blind for parachute landings. But now, as he gave orders for the searchlights to be switched off, he added instructions for a continued and increased alert with special attention being given to seaward. The odds against the MLs had always been cruelly high. Now they were virtually impossible. But no thought of turning back entered anyone's mind.

The most intricate part of the passage had now been reached, the channel winding between shallows. The *Campbeltown*'s draught gave her little or nothing under her keel. The slightest error and she would go aground. Once or twice, indeed, she was scraping through the mud, her speed checked to five knots, but her propellers churned her through. At 1.20 a.m. MGB 314, leading the force, passed the old disused tower of Les Morées in midstream. With less than two miles to go, all was still. The rain had stopped, and the moon was breaking intermittently through gaps in the overcast, easing the navigational problems. Ryder and Newman could hardly believe their good fortune.

But indeed, the sheer improbability of an enemy force brazenly appearing so far from home up such an impregnably fortified estuary was bluffing the defenders just as the planners had believed it would. The flotilla had been reported by lookouts on the east bank and again at 1.15 by the naval signal station opposite. Though the commander of the coast defence guns on receipt of this gave the order to stand by to attack naval targets, for the next five minutes telephone messages passed to and fro as the various authorities checked whether any German ships were expected. Not until 1.20 did a signal go out from Mecke's headquarters, 'Beware landing', and the full organisation for such an emergency begin to function. At 1.22 the force was suddenly starkly illuminated in the blue-white glare of the beam of a searchlight.

Yet for a few more minutes even now, bluff was to earn a respite. From the *Campbeltown*'s gaff fluttered the German ensign. German recognition signals had been studied and prepared. As hesitant and desultory fire from a few automatic guns broke out, the code signals were flashed at the challenging stations. The firing ceased, while the *Campbeltown*, working up speed to eighteen knots, began her death ride. At 1.28 the bluff was over. The shore line erupted in a blast of gunfire. The tall, bearded, unruffled Beattie had already ordered 'Hoist Battle Ensigns'. In the glare of massed searchlights, the swastika flag was seen to come fluttering down and at the masthead of the *Campbeltown* and from each of the little ships astern of her the White Ensign broke out. The quiet, moon-bathed estuary of a moment earlier now became a deafening bedlam of criss-crossing tracer shells, the boom of the big coastal guns, the sharper crack of the 75-mm, the bark and thump of twelve-pounders and mortars, the head-splitting staccato cough of Bofors and Oerlikons and the mad chatter of machine-guns.

The odds against survival of many of the MLs were theoretically astronomical, brilliantly illuminated as they were, terribly vulnerable and under such a volume of fire at point-blank range; but the violence of their reply was an unpleasant surprise to the gunners on shore. After three or four minutes, when none of the little ships had as yet received crippling damage, the German fire slackened and some of the searchlights went out. And all this time the flotilla was forging ahead towards its objective.

Some immunity was given to the MLs by the concentration of enemy fire on the *Campbeltown*, which was being smothered in shell-bursts and swept by a whistling storm of tracers. Beattie had cleared the open bridge and was conning the ship from the meagre shelter of the wheelhouse. A succession of helmsmen was killed at the wheel beside him, but not for a moment did he relax the utter concentration required to guide his racing ship correctly up the harbour and pick out the essential landmarks against the blinding glare of searchlights. The armed auxiliary anchored off the port loomed up suddenly close to starboard, but before she could come into action she was smothered by pompom fire from the MGB, still leading the way. Meanwhile the *Campbeltown*'s decks were becoming a shambles as her exposed gun crews were wiped out one after another. Between decks, too, in engine and boiler rooms, bullets which had penetrated her thin steel sides ricocheted round the spaces, causing casualties. Her machinery remained undamaged, however, and when a momentary glimpse of the lighthouse on the Old Mole gave Beattie his exact position to set her on her final course for the lock gates, she was doing twenty knots. With 700 yards to go he passed the warning, 'Stand by to ram' and everyone aboard braced themselves for the shock. The caisson was still invisible from the *Campbeltown*'s bridge. The ship was racing forward under such a concentration of fire that it seemed impossible for anyone to survive. On her forecastle a fire raged.

Then at 200 yards the caisson appeared, an indistinct black line below the glare of searchlight beams and Beattie knew he had brought his ship accurately to her target and her last resting place. There was a momentary check as she tore her way through the anti-torpedo net guarding the caisson. Then the ship seemed to gather herself together for a final effort. At 1.34 she smashed squarely into the centre of the caisson and shuddered to a standstill. Turning to Captain

R. K. Montgomery, Royal Engineers, commanding the demolition parties in the *Campbeltown*, Beattie said with a smile, 'Well, there we are. Four minutes late!'

It was the end of their mission for Beattie and his ship's company. They were free to take whatever chances of seeking safety remained open to them as soon as the military demolition parties and fighting troops who had come in the ship had been landed and dispatched to their assigned tasks – principally the destruction of the pumping station, the winding machinery of the two caissons and the inner caisson itself. Half the survivors landed over the forecastle and made their way, through continued heavy fire which caused further casualties, to MGB 314 which, according to plan, had landed the military commander and headquarters in the nearby Old Entrance of the port. The remainder, including Beattie, were embarked with their wounded in ML 177 which, having landed her Commandos at the Old Entrance, was brought alongside the *Campbeltown*'s quarter.

The *Campbeltown* had reached her assigned destination. But not unless and until the monstrous explosive charges in her bowels were detonated would her task have been completed. For the caisson was of much too stout a construction to be destroyed by ramming alone. The time fuses were set for 7 a.m. – five and a half hours ahead. While the acid was eating slowly through the copper in the fuses – or so it was hoped – deeds of peerless valour were taking place elsewhere.

Space does not permit any extensive account of heroic exploits of the various demolition parties and fighting troops of the Commandos – nor, indeed, is a book on Fighting Seamen the proper place for them. They can be read in all their details in C. E. Lucas Phillips' stirring book, *The Greatest Raid of All*. Before following the fortunes of the ships and their companies, however, it should be said that the demolition parties brought in the *Campbeltown* achieved brilliant and total success. When they had finished they had ensured that the great dry dock would be out of action for at least a year. None, however, were to escape, all being either killed or captured after a fight of the utmost gallantry.

Chance of escape for more than a handful vanished, in fact, very quickly as will be seen from the fate of the majority of the MLs. The launches in the port column carried troops destined for tasks in an area to seaward of the port and dry dock and were intended to be landed at a stone jetty known as the Old Mole. Those in the starboard column were to disembark their troops in the Old Entrance to the basin of the port. For clarity, the story of the two columns will be taken separately, starting with the starboard.

The petrol-laden, wooden craft enjoyed at first an astonishing immunity partly attributable to the enemy's concentration on the *Campbeltown*. There was one total loss before the ramming, however. When abreast of the Old Mole, ML 192, Lieutenant-Commander W. L. Stephens in command, was wrecked by two direct hits and set ablaze. Out of control, she swung to port, careered through the port column and crashed into the sea wall. The quay was fourteen feet above the heads of the crew so that it was impossible to get ashore. The wounded were put aboard a Carley raft before abandon ship was ordered. Drowning accounted for many of the heavily encumbered Commandos, all but five of whom were lost. Those and most of the ship's company, including Stephens, were taken prisoner.

The next boat in the line, ML 262, commanded by Lieutenant E. A. Burt, escaped serious damage during the approach, as did Lieutenant E. H. Beart's ML 267 following him. Blinded by the searchlights, both overshot their assigned landing place in the Old Entrance so that by the time they had turned round and retraced their steps, the fourth and sixth in the column had already played their initial parts. The fourth boat, ML 268, heading for the Old Entrance, had drawn a smothering fire on herself. In a few seconds she was ablaze from bow to stern and very soon she blew up, spewing blazing petrol on the surface of the water. Her captain, Lieutenant A. B. K. Tillie, survived, but few others aboard her did so. The sixth boat was ML 177 which we have seen alongside the *Campbeltown*'s quarter, embarking her survivors. From his position at the rear of the line, her captain, Lieutenant M. F. Rodier, was confronted, by the time his turn to approach the port had come, with a scene of death and destruction to daunt the bravest heart. Tillie's boat had blown up. To port of him two launches of the other column were burning. Ahead of him ML 156 had staggered out of the line, obviously with many casualties. Through it all, Rodier drove steadily forward and landed his soldiers in the Old Entrance. Then, having picked up the *Campbeltown* survivors, he headed seawards, miraculously unharmed. His little ship, with more than forty men, was crowded, to say the least. Many were wounded and Surgeon-Lieutenant Winthrop, the *Campbeltown*'s doctor, with Mr Hargreaves the torpedo-gunner helping, had his hands full. On the tiny bridge, the imperturbable Beattie joined Rodier.

From the comparative darkness under the sea walls of the entrance, ML 177 had emerged into the white glare of a dozen searchlights and the storm of shells and bullets from scores of automatic weapons. Even though Rodier jinked and swerved skilfully it was still a miracle that his boat was not seriously damaged. He paused to fire his torpedoes at some ill-defined targets before, under the cover of a screen from his white smoke-making apparatus, he fled at full speed downriver. Such luck could not last, though. He still had to run the gauntlet of the batteries of heavier guns on both banks of the river lower down. As ML 177 ran out of range of the automatic weapons, the 75-mm took up the challenge. For another three miles the launch ran, jinking from side to side before the end came as a shell burst in the engine room. Beattie left the bridge to see what could be done and at that moment a second shell hit it. It was the end of the road for Rodier, who was mortally wounded and died in a few minutes.

The launch was now on fire fore and aft. Wooden construction and petrol made a fatal combination. Yet for three hours the crew fought the flames as the boat drifted seawards on the current before the order was given to abandon ship. On the one remaining Carley raft some of the wounded were embarked. The remainder had to take to the water. Few were the survivors. Of the *Campbeltown*'s officers, only Beattie and Mr Locke, the Warrant Engineer, made the shore where they were taken prisoner. One or two others, including Petty Officer Stocker, Chief Boatswain's Mate of the destroyer, were able to clamber aboard the wreck of the troopship *Lancastria* sunk in the estuary at the time of the fall of France in 1940.

Now let us return to follow the fortunes of the two launches commanded by Burt and Beart which also landed their troops as planned in the Old Entrance. By the time they reached it the enemy had mustered a great many machine-guns and automatic weapons to concentrate on the restricted area in which the launches were forced to manoeuvre. Beart's ML was quickly overwhelmed and set ablaze, Beart himself being killed, and it had to be abandoned. Burt was luckier, for a time. He was able to withdraw into open water after completing his mission and make off downstream. Though his launch was riddled and had suffered a number of casualties, it might now have been able to escape seaward; but off the Old Mole, Burt saw ML 457, commanded by his friend, Lieutenant T. A. M. Collier, one of the port column which had successfully landed her Commandos, lying disabled and under heavy fire. Collier, lying on the bridge mortally wounded, had just given the order to abandon ship. With selfless gallantry Burt took his craft alongside to take his friend off.

'I've had it, Ted,' Collier objected, 'get out quick before the bastards get you, too.'

There was, indeed, nothing that could be done for Collier or his crew. Burt sheered off to resume his bid for safety; but it was too late. The pause had been fatal. A storm of shell hit his boat, smashing her up and causing many casualties. She drifted away helplessly on the current, burning, to be finally abandoned. Once again there were few survivors to tell the tale, but Burt himself, carried away downstream, reached the Les Morées tower where he was picked up by the Germans the following day.

Another in the starboard column was Lieutenant N. R. Nock's spare ML 298. With no troops embarked, his duty was to draw the enemy's fire, engage his guns and searchlights and (it had been optimistically planned) to pick up troops on their withdrawal. All these he gallantly fulfilled, except that he found no troops to embark; and, by picking a spot out of the searchlight glare from which to fight, he avoided serious damage until the time came to escape. Then, as he moved out into the open to try to rescue survivors of other boats from the bullet-lashed and fire-covered water, his craft was set ablaze. The searchlight beams settled on her. Several of the crew were killed and Nock himself wounded, but with the coxswain, Petty Officer Hambley, at the wheel, she limped away downstream only to disintegrate as both engines exploded simultaneously. Nock and Hambley survived to be taken prisoners, but very few besides.

So the tragic tale continued. Escape from the hellish storm of shot under the cruel glare of the searchlights was wellnigh impossible. Yet two launches of the starboard column did win clear. ML 156, fifth in line, made two attempts to get into the Old Entrance to land her party of Commandos, but, obstructed by the crippled boats in front, one engine knocked out and steering gear smashed, her captain, Lieutenant L. Fenton, severely wounded, she was forced to give up the attempt. Nevertheless it was not until 2.30 a.m. when casualties and damage had dissipated all hope of achieving anything, that the decision was taken to withdraw. On one engine and steering by hand, ML 156 succeeded in repassing the batteries lining the estuary and gained the open sea.

The other craft which survived the inferno was Lieutenant T. W. Boyd's ML 160 which had actually led the starboard column into action. Having no Commandos to land, her task was to fire her torpedoes at any suitable target and to give supporting fire wherever it was needed. Thus ML 160 was continually in the thick of things and yet managed to escape being entirely crippled. When the time came to withdraw, Boyd first rescued the survivors from ML 447 off the Old Mole and stopped to pick up, under heavy fire, some more men from the water before heading seawards, zigzagging slowly down river on one engine to reach the open sea and safety.

Appalling as had been the cost, the task assigned to the launches of the starboard column, the disembarkation of their troops at the Old Entrance, had been to a great extent successful. The port column, whose point of disembarkation had been the Old Mole, had met disaster at a much earlier stage and few of their troops were disembarked. But before we go there, we must see what happened to the two other craft in the Old Entrance – the headquarters MGB carrying the two force commanders and Wynn's MTB 74.

The former, having seen the *Campbeltown*'s spectacular arrival, was taken in and Colonel Newman and his staff disembarked to set up their headquarters ashore. The MGB then took on board those survivors of the destroyer's crew who had disembarked from her forecastle on to the caisson. At the same time Wynn arrived with his craft. The *Campbeltown*'s success had made a further attack on the caisson unnecessary, as Ryder ascertained by a thorough inspection. He, therefore, told Wynn to fire his 'torpedoes' at the lockgates of the Old Entrance, after which he was to embark as many *Campbeltown* survivors as possible and escape.

The huge charges duly laid at the base of the lock-gates, Wynn's little craft, very overcrowded, turned to leave, nosed her way out into the stream and set off with a roar of her five engines at some forty knots. At that speed she was too difficult a target for the enemy guns and she had soon left the inferno behind her. The open sea and safety lay close ahead. Then suddenly, ahead of her, Wynn saw a Carley raft with two men on it. He stopped at once to pick them up and in doing so threw away his chance of escape. For out of the darkness stabbed a searchlight. A heavy gun on the shore flashed and a shell hit the little ship amidships. Wynn was knocked unconscious. Around him the MGB was going up in a blaze of petrol-soaked timbers. His crew had abandoned ship – all but one. Chief Motor Mechanic W. H. Lovegrove, painfully wounded, had achieved a miracle of tireless improvisation in keeping the temperamental engines of his unorthodox craft functioning and in repairing them under withering fire. To this record of steadfast conduct he now added an act of self-sacrificing courage that puts him amongst the immortal heroes.

Fighting his way through the flames to his young captain, he lifted the helpless figure in his arms, dragged him into the water and swam with him to a Carley raft. For twelve hours, as the raft drifted downstream and the thirty or so men clinging to it dropped away one by one to die, Lovegrove supported his captain. By dawn only four men remained, Wynn, Lovegrove, Petty Officer Robert Ward and Stoker William Savage. Lovegrove and Savage climbed aboard the raft and hauled Wynn up to join them. Ward would not follow, but remained in the water trying to push the raft in front of him as he swam, only to collapse suddenly and vanish under the water. The little trio remaining was picked up at last by a German gunboat and taken prisoner.

That of all the craft which had come into the Old Entrance only one had survived to reach the sea was unknown to Ryder until he, after Wynn's boat had left, ordered Lieutenant D. M. C. Curtis, commanding the MGB, to move out into the river so that he might see how things were going at the Old Mole. Then for the first time he saw the daunting scene of burning launches. For besides the five boats of the starboard column which had been destroyed, two more from the other column had suffered the same fate. These were Lieutenant T. D. L. Platt's ML 447, the rescue of whose crew by Boyd's launch has been recounted, and ML 457 in

49

which we have seen the heroic end of her young captain, Lieutenant Collier. The remainder, much damaged and with many casualties, succeeded in extricating themselves and making the open sea, carrying their Commandos with them.

Ryder quickly appreciated that things had gone seriously awry at the Old Mole where the enemy had proved to be in such strong force that few of the Commandos got ashore and those that did so were able to achieve little before being captured. At Ryder's orders the MGB was taken in to try to restore the situation with her fairly powerful gun armament, but though her gun crews performed prodigies it was not enough. His boat, riddled with shot and under the concentration of a host of guns, was soon the only one left afloat in the vicinity. Nothing remained for him but to try to tell Newman that the plan for withdrawal had collapsed and with this in mind he returned towards the Old Entrance only to find that the landing places were now in enemy hands. The seamen could do no more in the enterprise. It remained only to withdraw if they could. At twenty-four knots the MGB turned downriver to make good her escape.

So the river battle came to an end. Nine out of the seventeen small craft taking part had been destroyed. It might have been thought that, once clear of the estuary and its defences, the remainder could count on reaching safety under the protection of the *Atherstone* and *Tynedale*, waiting for them at a rendezvous to seaward. One more was to be lost, however, its end being perhaps the most heroic of all.

ML 306, commanded by Lieutenant Ian B. Henderson, had been last but one in the port column. By the time his turn had come to go alongside the Old Mole, it was plainly an impossibility and after a tentative effort to do so, he had swung away with the intention of landing his Commando troops at the Old Entrance instead. There, like Ryder, he found the landing places so strongly held by the enemy that it was suicidal to enter and murderous to put the soldiers ashore. Withdrawal was the only thing left. The Fates were preserving the little company for an illustrious destiny and on their passage seaward they escaped damage though constantly drenched by the spray from shell splashes leaping up alongside them.

ML 306 reached the open sea too early for the planned rendezvous with the destroyers and by 5.30 a.m. was jogging along at slow speed waiting for dawn, when in the darkness ahead blacker shapes were sighted against the skyline. As they loomed larger it was evident that they must be enemy ships and that they must pass very close on an opposite course. The ML's engines were stopped and in deathly silence all hands awaited the outcome, hoping that in the blackness they would not be seen.

The ships in fact were the five destroyer-minesweepers which had been sent to sea as a result of the report of U-593. They were now returning to harbour. They filed by the ML barely a hundred yards away, so close, indeed, that the voices of the German crew could be heard. Three of the ships passed and no alarm had been raised. Henderson and his crew, their weapons at the ready, began to hope. Then the third ship was seen suddenly to sheer out of line and circle back. A searchlight flashed on and the ML, its White Ensign standing out clearly, was starkly illuminated.

The impossible odds facing the crew of the little motor launch would have made surrender no shame. But the spirit in which all hands had gone into the 'sauciest job since Drake' was still animating them, and with the sailors were the fighting Commandos, bitterly conscious that they had been forced to retreat without striking a blow, leaving their comrades ashore fighting for their lives. From every weapon on board the ML fire spewed forth. There followed a wild, unequal fight lasting nearly an hour, in which the German ship, the *Jaguar*, after an initial unsuccessful attempt to ram the launch, circled and steadily cut her to pieces with her automatic weapons, while the answering fusillade from the launch's crew and the Commandos – by no means ineffective – gradually died away as one by one they were killed or wounded.

Twice the Germans ceased firing to call upon the British to surrender. They were answered by bursts of machine-gun fire from the dauntless Commandos, wounded and dying as most of them were. The end could not be long delayed, however, and when the *Jaguar* again came alongside the launch her guns were at last silent. Henderson had been killed and it was left to Lieutenant Swayne, commanding the soldiers, to make the surrender.

So ended a 'last stand' as heroic as any in naval or military annals. How near ML 306 had been to reaching safety! For while her fight with the *Jaguar* was going on, the remainder of the German flotilla had had a brief engagement with the *Tynedale*, an engagement which the Germans did not press in spite of their superiority of force.

Of the seven surviving British small craft, three failed to make contact with the destroyers and returned to England independently. The remaining four – three MLs and the MGB – having transferred their wounded to the *Atherstone*, began the journey home with her and the *Tynedale* but had eventually to be scuttled. The MGB from which Commander Ryder climbed aboard the *Atherstone* miraculously unhurt had not another man unwounded amongst her crew or the *Campbeltown*'s men she carried. The cost in lives of Operation 'Chariot' had indeed been high. The long ordeal of the motor craft, for all its roll of gallant deeds, makes painful reading. So let us turn to see what was achieved by so much valour and self-sacrifice.

Back in St Nazaire, as the gallant fight of Newman's Commandos came to its inevitable end soon after daylight on the morning of Saturday, 28 March, the Germans were able to look around at the results of the raid. They saw with dismay the wreckage of the pumping station and the winding houses which would make the great dry dock unusable for a long while to come. Nevertheless the damage was repairable and, so it seemed to them, the attempt to wreck the caisson had failed. Examination of the *Campbeltown* revealed no explosive charge. She could no doubt be towed away in due course. Interrogation of the captured Commandos revealed nothing, though the soldiers were bitterly disappointed that the hour had long passed at which the destroyer should have blown up. It was 10.35 a.m. and the *Campbeltown* was crowded with German officers and their ladies roaming through the ship, gazing curiously at the damage above and below decks and wondering contemptuously if the British could have thought that so flimsy a ship would burst the massive caisson. A moment later their doubts were answered in one cataclysmic explosion in which more than two hundred men and women were blown to pieces. It was followed by the roar of a cataract of water rushing into the empty dock, carrying with it the stern half of the *Campbeltown* and wrecking the two tankers inside the dock.

A wave of deep satisfaction swept through the captured Commandos and sailors still under interrogation, a satisfaction given piquancy by the consternation and even panic which seized their captors. The great sacrifice had not been made in vain.

One more shock remained for the Germans. Unknown to them, at the base of the lock-gates of the Old Entrance, lay the two explosive charges from Wynn's MTB, their fuses slowly working. By Monday afternoon, after a night of nervous tension, things had begun to calm down and the local commanders were preparing to face the inquiry which had been ordered by the enraged Führer. At 4.30 p.m. a fresh explosion as the first of Wynn's torpedoes went up, followed by a second an hour later, brought bewilderment and fear back in full flood amongst the shaken German troops. There followed a night of panic-stricken indiscipline as trigger-happy soldiers opened fire at shadows and German fired on German.

So ended Operation 'Chariot' – a deed of splendid valour, ranking with any in naval and military history for its successful achievements as well as for the gallantry with which it was performed.

7 Battling through to Malta

Hugh Popham, Arthur Thorpe and Anthony Kimmins

All through 1942 Malta was under vigorous attack. So strong was the enemy opposition that it became almost impossible for a time to get merchant ships to the island with essential supplies. By the beginning of August the position was desperate. And so the government ordered that the next convoy must take first place above every other naval operation anywhere in the world. Such was Malta's value.

That was why on 10 August 1942 fourteen merchant ships passed through the Straits of Gibraltar escorted by no less than the battleships *Nelson* and *Rodney*, the aircraft carriers *Victorious*, *Indomitable*, *Eagle* and *Furious*, the cruisers *Sirius*, *Phoebe*, *Charybdis*, *Kenya*, *Nigeria*, *Manchester* and *Cairo* – the whole supported by thirty-two destroyers. Forty-five warships in all to protect fourteen cargo vessels, such was the weight of opposition expected! The action was code-named Operation Pedestal.

The convoy endured a running battle for most of its passage. During the trip, the carrier *Eagle* was hit, an event witnessed by Lieutenant (A) Hugh Popham, RNVR, who was a pilot aboard the *Indomitable*. He described what he saw in *Sea Flight*.

The wind was chancy, and we were to be boosted off. I was in position on the catapult, engine running. The flight deck engineer waggled the ailerons to draw my attention to something or other, and I looked out over the port side to see what he wanted. And, as I did so, I stared in shocked surprise beyond him to where *Eagle* was steaming level with us, half a mile away. For as I turned, smoke and steam suddenly poured from her, she took on a heavy list to port, and the air shook with a series of muffled explosions.

Over the sound of the engine, I yelled: '*Eagle*'s been hit!'

Listing to port, she swung outwards in a slow, agonised circle, and in seven minutes turned abruptly over. For a few seconds longer her bottom remained visible; and then the trapped air in her hull escaped, and with a last gust of steam and bubbles she vanished. All that remained was the troubled water, a spreading stain of oil and the clustered black dots of her ship's company.

There had hardly been time to assimilate the fact that she had been hit before she had capsized and sunk; and when I took off a few minutes later my mind was still numbed by what I had seen. It had come so completely without forewarning. Our thoughts had been focused on the idea of air attack; we had never dreamed that a U-boat would slip through the screen of destroyers to attack with such chilling precision. It was as if, at any moment, our own ship might stagger and lurch and list, and our aircraft go slithering down the deck into the sea.

In the air we saw the whole fleet alter course, while the destroyers hounded back and forth, dropping depth charges. The loss of *Eagle* had screwed up the tension by another full turn, and we flew our patrol with tingling nerves. And still the expected raids did not come.

The day wore on. At 20.00 hours Brian and I were back on standby. The sky was gaudy with the first high colours of sunset. In an hour and a half it would be dark, and readiness would be over for the day. We hung about on the flight deck, Mae Wests on, helmets round our necks, gloves in sticky hands.

'Another forty minutes,' Brian said, 'and I should think we can call it a day.'

The Tannoy crackled. 'Scramble the Hurricanes. Scramble the Hurricanes!'

The fitters in the cockpits pressed the starter buttons, and the four Merlins opened up with a blast of sound and a gust of blue smoke. As we scrambled up the wings, the crew hopped out the other side, fixing our straps with urgent fingers. Connect RT; switch on ten degrees of flap. Trim.

Quick cockpit check. The ship was under full helm, racing up into wind – and we were off and climbing at full boost on a northerly vector to 20 000 feet, head swivelling. Down to 12 000; alter course; climb to 20 000 again. And there they were, a big formation of 88s below us. One after another we peeled off and went down after them. They broke formation as they saw us coming, and Brian and I picked one and went after him. He turned and dived away, and we stuffed the nose down, full bore, willing our aircraft to make up on him. At extreme range we gave him a long burst; bits came off and smoke poured out of one engine, and then he vanished into the thickening twilight. We hadn't a hope of catching him and making sure; already he had led us away from the convoy, and so, cursing our lack of speed, we reformed, joined up with Steve and Paddy, the other members of the flight, and started to climb back to base.

The sight we saw took our breath away. The light was slowly dying, and the ships were no more than a pattern on the grey steel plate of the sea; but where we had left them sailing peaceably through the sunset, now they were enclosed in a sparkling net of tracer and bursting shells, a mesh of fire. Every gun in fleet and convoy was firing, and the darkling air was laced with threads and beads of flame.

For a time we hunted round the fringes of it, hoping to catch somebody coming out; but the light was going, and we were running short of petrol. We had already been in the air for an hour, most of it with the throttle wide open. There was no sign of the 88s which had started it all; and it was not clear at first what the ships were still firing at. Then we saw the tracer coming morsing up towards us, and one or two black puffs of smoke burst uncomfortably close. We moved round the fleet, and the bursts followed us; and the truth could no longer be disregarded. They were firing at anything that flew.

We pulled away out of range, and called up the ship and asked for instructions. Stewart Morris's voice was never calmer or more sweetly reasonable than at that moment.

'Stand by, Yellow Flight. Will pancake you as soon as possible.'

'If you'd stop shooting at us it would be a help,' Brian said, without eliciting a reply.

We closed the convoy again, to test their mood, and provoked another hail of gunfire. We tried switching on navigation lights, which merely encouraged them to improve on their earlier efforts. Disheartened, we withdrew.

By now it was beginning to get dark, and in the gloom I lost the others. With the prospect of a night deck-landing at the end of it all, the situation was beginning to lose its attractions.

'Check fuel, Yellow Flight'; the urbanity of Stewart's voice gave one a sudden, sharp yearning to be back on the familiar deck. Worlds seemed to divide the dark cockpit and its glowing instruments from the dark air direction room, with its glowing screens, worlds of twilight sky and sea, as black now as well-water, and the spasmodic bursts of fire.

I tested the gauges of the three tanks, and found I had less than twenty gallons left, a bare half hour's flying. On my own now, I throttled right back, cut the revs, went into fully weak mixture. It looked as if those eighteen gallons were going to have to last a long time.

Every now and then I approached the ships, still just visible below; and each time the guns opened up. At last, I dropped down to fifty feet, and ploughed slowly up and down between the screen and the convoy, waiting for a chance to find the ship, and hoping to find her into wind. From time to time one of the merchant ships on one side – they had thoughtfully been provided with four Bofors guns each against just such an opportunity – or the destroyers on the other side would spot me, and the red dots of their tracer would come drifting up at me. Once something bigger hit the water with a splash alongside, and I jerked away, frightened and angry. It was at about this point that my RT decided to pack up.

I was down to ten gallons, and began to go over in my

mind the procedure for ditching, for if I wasn't shot down, and if I didn't find a deck to land on very soon, I should surely have to land in the sea. I jettisoned the hood and released my parachute harness and kept ducking the gusts of gunfire and came, all at once, to the sudden, stabbing realisation that this might be the end of me. Up to that exact instant, flying up and down between the dark lanes of ships, I hadn't thought of it like that. Now it hit me, as blindly bruising as hatred, as confusing as a blow. I didn't know how I was going to get back aboard: now, for the first time, it seemed highly probable that I should not, and I understood the implications. I didn't wholly accept them; there was still a loophole or two through which the mind went bravely peering, past the dead-end of the inimical night.

Automatically I checked the tanks. Five gallons. The time had come for desperate measures unless I was going to accept without an effort my own approaching death. I flew in low over the convoy, disregarding the squalls of fire, in search of a ship to land on. It was now 21.30 hours, and quite dark, and the first one I chose turned out to have a funnel amidships. I sheered off hurriedly, and just managed to make out what looked like a carrier astern of the convoy. I made for it, dropping hook, wheels and flaps on the way. It was difficult to see what she was doing: then I caught the glimmer of her wake, and began my approach. There wasn't a light showing; but I could see by the wake that she was under helm. Would she be into wind in time?

I steadied into the approach, and a pair of lighted bats materialised on her deck and began mechanically to wave me round. I checked my petrol for the last time. All the tanks were reading 'o'. There was a slight chance I might get down in one piece, even with the deck swinging: there was no chance of my getting round again. I continued my approach.

The batsman's signals were becoming a little feverish; but now I could see the deck, swerving away to starboard under me. It was my last chance. I crammed the nose down, cut the throttle, and with the last bit of extra speed, tried to kick the aircraft into a turn to match the ship's. She was swinging too fast. The wheels touched, and the skid wiped off the undercarriage and the aircraft hit the deck and slithering and screeching up towards the island on its belly. I hung on and waited. It stopped at last, just short of the island, on the centre-line — what was left of it.

For a fraction of a second I was too relieved to move. And then, out of the corner of my eye, I saw a tongue of blue flame flicker across the bottom of the cockpit, and I yanked the pin out of the straps and was over the side. An instant later the wreck went up in a haze of flame.

It seemed excessively ignorant to have to ask which ship I was in; and so I waited in the doorway into the island while the fire crews doused the blaze, and Jumbo the crane lurched up and removed the bits. (The ship was *Victorious*.)

'Did anyone see the pilot?' I heard close beside me.

'No. Did you?'

'I haven't seen him. Wasn't still in the cockpit, was he?'

'No.'

'Well, either he must have made a ruddy quick getaway, or the kite must have landed-on by itself.'

I didn't feel particularly like advertising myself, but I had to settle this.

'It's all right,' I said diffidently. 'I was the pilot.'

They both looked at me.

Eagle had been hit by four torpedoes fired by U-73. Though she sank quickly, 930 of her 1160 crew survived. Arthur Thorpe, an *Exchange Telegraph* reporter, was one of the men who escaped; his account appeared in the *Daily Telegraph* on 14 August.

We scrambled up the ladder to the upper deck with the ship listing over terrifyingly to the port side on which we were. The sea, normally ten feet below the rails, was surging ominously a bare two feet below them. We made the quarterdeck and grabbed anything we could to haul ourselves up the steeply sloping deck to the starboard side. Clutching the bulletproof casing enclosing the quarterdeck, I found myself next to a first lieutenant who was blowing up a lifebelt. I followed suit.

Looking round I saw the deck slanting more sharply than a gabled roof. Six-inch shells weighing over 100 lb tore loose from their brackets and bumped down the cliff-like deck. Ratings on the port side saw them coming and flung themselves into the water to escape injury. Foolishly I asked the first lieutenant, 'Is she going?' He nodded. Several ratings, grasping the casing, clambered towards us. They fastened a stout rope to the deck. They slithered down into the thick oil welling out under the ship and coating the sea and drifted away. With perfect confidence in my lifebelt I did the same and let go.

I went under the wave but when I came to the surface I realised with horror that I had not put enough air into the lifebelt. My head was barely above water. With all the poor swimmer's dread of deep water I splashed and kicked clear of the ship. As I got free of the oil patch the sea became choppy and every wave washed clear over my head till I was dizzy. I gave myself up for lost.

No wreckage was near which I could grasp. Then as a wave lifted me I saw a glorious sight – a cork float twenty yards off with sailors clinging round it. I fought madly to reach it. Three times my head went under and then I saw the float a few feet away. I snatched despairingly but missed. Making another wild clutch, I felt my fingers grip.

Half a dozen ratings holding on tried to loosen the ropes to open the cork raft out. It was tied up like a round bundle. But the oil on their fingers made the task impossible. The water was quite warm, but I had difficulty in holding on firmly owing to my oil-smothered hands. Another rating swam up and caught hold too. He told us his leg was broken. We helped him to crawl on to the centre of the bundle. The waves broke over us. I pulled myself up and saw the *Eagle* 200 yards away, lying on her side. Down the great red expanse of the *Eagle*'s hull men like ants were sliding down into the sea.

Suddenly I felt a shock at the base of my spine. I knew it was a depth charge from a destroyer hunting the U-boat responsible. 'She is going,' gasped one of the men. Then came a mighty rumbling as the sea poured relentlessly into the *Eagle*, forcing out the air. The water threshed over her in a fury of white foam and then subsided. She had gone.

Thorpe was killed later while still serving as a war correspondent with the Royal Navy.

Of the escorting vessels *Eagle*, *Manchester*, *Cairo*, and the destroyer *Foresight* were lost on the way to Malta; only five of the fourteen merchantmen arrived. One of the cargo ships was the *Ohio*, whose valiance was remembered by Commander Anthony Kimmins in an article published in *The Listener* on 27 August 1942.

She had been uppermost in our thoughts from the moment we sailed, for she was a tanker carrying the most important and most dangerous cargo of all, and so very conspicuous from the air with her funnel right aft. Her name was *Ohio*, an American-built ship manned by a British crew, skippered be a very great man called Captain Mason. It was obvious that she would be a special target for the enemy and sure enough she was hit by a torpedo at the same time as we were.

She was forced to stop, and later, as we went up alongside in the *Ashanti*, another merchantman was blazing not far off. It was that night when things weren't looking too good. Admiral Burrough hailed her from the bridge. 'I've got to go on with the rest of the convoy. Make the shore route if you can and slip across to Malta. They need you badly.' The reply was instantaneous. 'Don't worry, sir, we'll do our best. Good luck.'

By next morning, by some superhuman effort, they had got the engines going and had caught us up in spite of having lost their compass and having to steer from aft. She then took station on our quarter and *Ohio*'s next bit of trouble was when a Stuka attacking us was hit fair and square and crashed right into her.

For the rest of the forenoon she was always picked out for special attention, and time and time again she completely disappeared amongst the clouds of water from bursting bombs. But again and again she came through. Then at last one hit her. She was set on fire, but after a terrific fight they managed to get the flames under control. Her engines had been partly wrecked, but she just managed to make two knots and plodded on. Destroyers left to look after her, but later she was hit again and her engines finally put out of action. Then they took her in tow, but the tow parted. During the night with the help of a minesweeper from Malta they got her a further twenty miles. All next day she was again continuously bombed and towing became impossible. But that night she reached Malta.

Admiral Burrough's last signal to *Ohio* was short and to the point: 'I'm proud to have met you.'

8 Submarine 'Wahoo'

Donald MacIntyre

The British Far East Fleet may have suffered at the hands of the Japanese (see chapter 5) but that did not prevent the Royal Navy operating in the Pacific and Indian oceans. Far from it. British seamen worked there in support of the American fleet. One very busy vessel was the U.S. submarine *Wahoo*, which, towards the end of 1942, was put under the command of Lieutenant-Commander Dudley W. Morton. Morton's story, told by Donald MacIntyre in *Fighting Under the Sea*, typifies the kind of life submariners lived in those days, the dangers they endured, their courage and suffering.

The successful fighting submariner may be one of a number of differing types. The dedicated, earnest patriot who can impart his own sense of purpose and duty into his crew will be one. The irascible disciplinarian may be another and may even get the devotion of his crew if he is human enough to recognise his own shortcomings. Yet another type and the most lovable is the cheerful extrovert who can meet danger and hardship with a laugh and a wisecrack, giving an impression of absolute fearlessness; who can renew his men's courage and fortitude by his light-hearted example though perhaps beneath the unconcerned exterior he may be just as normally fearful as they. Such a one was Lieutenant-Commander Dudley W. Morton, known to his many friends as 'Mush', short for 'Mushmouth', earned by his reputation as a spinner of yarns.

Mush Morton assumed command of the submarine *Wahoo* at the end of 1942 after her second patrol during which he had been embarked to gain experience. The Engineer Officer of the *Wahoo* at this time was Lieutenant George Grider who has written revealingly of his shipmates and with an affection amounting to hero-worship of Morton shining through every word of the early chapters of his book of personal memoirs, *War Fish*. Under their first skipper, Lieutenant-Commander W. G. Kennedy, the *Wahoo*'s crew had been brought to a high pitch of efficiency under a strict regime and had been 'blooded' during their second patrol by the sinking of a Japanese transport in the approaches to Rabaul. Morton's less rigid attitude to rules of discipline and his informality of manner with subordinates applied to this well-trained ship's company was to make them a veritable band of brothers.

At the same time he himself was possessed of an uninhibited craving for action, the effect of which on him, in Grider's word, was that 'Joy welled out of him. His voice remained the same but his eyes lit up with a delight ... his supreme joy was literally to seek out and destroy the enemy.'

The combination of such a skipper and such a crew was bound to result in brilliant achievements so long as a fair portion of good luck was granted them. It is not to be wondered at that the *Wahoo* was to build up a tremendous reputation and that at least two of Morton's officers, his executive officer Richard O'Kane and George Grider, were to go on to achieve brilliant careers of their own as submarine skippers, the former winning the Congressional Medal of Honor.

Mush Morton's first patrol in command was to set the pattern for *Wahoo*'s subsequent career. Assigned to a patrol area off Palau, orders were received *en route* to reconnoitre Wewak Harbour on the north-east coast of New Guinea. To a man like Morton this meant nothing less than going right inside. The fact that no chart of the place, even a small-scale one, was carried did not deter him. A machinist produced from his locker a school atlas on which Wewak was marked. Using his camera as an enlarger, Grider 'blew up' the relevant portion of the map and traced a rough outline of the harbour. With this, which of course gave no indication of depths of water or details of any reefs or shoals, Morton cheerfully shaped course for the anchorage, the entrance to which was sheltered by two islands, one of which, appropriately enough, was named Mushu.

In the first grey light of dawn on 24 January 1943, the two islands were identified from three miles to seaward. The *Wahoo* submerged and steered for the passage between them. By the time it was reached the sun was up. From the entrance the inner harbour was hidden at the end of a nine-mile, dogleg channel. To investigate it would entail navigating submerged among unknown hazards, relying upon the changing colour of the water to give warning of coral reefs, but this did not daunt Mush Morton.

It was typical of his unorthodox methods and trust in his subordinates that he did not himself man the periscope during action, leaving his executive officer to do this while he took general control in the conning tower. Thus it was Dick O'Kane who, as the submarine nosed cautiously into the channel, reported two torpedo boats heading for sea. Though as Morton noted in his report, 'This was encouraging because patrol boats were likely to mean shipping', they were too small fry for him and he ducked down and kept out of their way until they had passed. Nothing more came in sight in that stretch of water, except for a small tug in the far distance with a barge alongside.

The rest of the morning was spent nosing this way and that, charting the shadows discovered and noting any prominent guide points. The sheer impudence of trying to feel his way without aid of charts into an enemy stronghold appealed to Morton's love of taking risks. His gaiety transmitted itself to everyone in the conning tower, particularly O'Kane, a kindred spirit. On several occasions the submarine came near to grounding but even these incidents failed to mar their boyish enjoyment of the adventure. Then about noon, above the palm trees of one of the islands, the masthead of a large ship was sighted. Trying to get at it, Morton found his way barred by a reef.

He backed away and pressed on down the main channel and as he rounded a corner, O'Kane reported a large destroyer at anchor. Six miles inside an enemy harbour in glassy calm, perilously translucent though fortunately deep water, he never hesitated as to what he should do – attack! Dead slow, rigged for silent running, the *Wahoo* crept forward. At brief intervals O'Kane ordered the periscope raised and reported the situation. At 6000 yards' range Morton passed the stand-by order to the tubes. A few minutes later the periscope slid up to give O'Kane a final sight of the target. His startled cry told of a total change in the situation. The destroyer had got under way and was headed out.

Whether the *Wahoo*'s periscope had been sighted breaking the mirror-like surface of the water or the Japanese ship was merely putting to sea, Morton could not tell. Either way, he intended to attack. Turning at right angles to starboard to get to one side of the destroyer's track, he prepared to fire his stern tubes as she crossed astern; but when next O'Kane raised the periscope he found that the enemy had also turned and was now heading across the bow. New settings for a bow shot were hastily calculated. At 3000 yards three torpedoes were fired, steam torpedoes trailing a broad white wake which the enemy could not fail to see. There was nothing to be gained by lowering the periscope. O'Kane watched them – all missing astern! The estimation of fifteen knots speed of the enemy had been too low. Quickly adjusting for twenty knots, Morton ordered a fourth fired. But by now the destroyer was turning away, avoiding the torpedo and then continuing the circle to come round to a course for an attack that simply could not fail.

Two more torpedoes remained in the fore tubes. To direct them at the target needed no complicated calculation for she was now racing directly for the *Wahoo*'s periscope. At 1800 yards the first was fired 'down the throat'. O'Kane saw it miss. Watching the oncoming destroyer growing rapidly larger in his sights, Dick O'Kane calmly asked when he should fire the last one. 'When it fills four divisions'* came the reply. 'It already fills eight!' yelled O'Kane. 'Then for God's sake, fire!' shouted Morton, for once shaken out of his composure. At point-blank range the torpedo shot away and at the same moment the order was given to 'Take her down'.

Morton dared not order a greater depth than ninety feet for fear of striking the rocky bottom. As they planed down all hands cowered waiting for the first depth charge. There came one explosion loud and close, shaking the boat. They waited for the next. Nothing came, no explosion, no roar of passing propellers. Someone whispered, 'Maybe *we hit him!*' With a laugh of pure enjoyment, Morton ordered 'periscope depth'. As the periscope broke the surface the destroyer was seen to be stopped with the whole of her bow blown off, and her crew running hither and thither in total confusion. Grider's camera recorded the scene through the periscope and the remainder of the crew were given the chance to see their handiwork before the *Wahoo* left the scene, hastened by an aerial bomb which fell close by.

It is not surprising that the spirits of the *Wahoo*'s crew were riding on the crest of the wave after such contemptuous treatment of a destroyer, the submarine's most feared opponent. Memory of the narrowness of their escape had been banished by the gay confidence of Morton and O'Kane. Two days later there came fresh cause for high spirits.

By this time the *Wahoo* had taken up her assigned patrol position south of the Western Caroline Islands on the important Japanese supply route between Palau and the Bismarck Archipelago. 26 January 1943 had dawned warm, clear and calm so that a wisp of smoke betraying a ship beyond the horizon was clearly to be seen. Remaining on the surface Morton steered for it and as the masts of two freighters were raised, he shaped course to get ahead of them where

* Divisions of the scale superimposed on the periscope's lens.

he submerged and lay in wait. As the target approached, he was surprised to see that they were steaming unescorted and on a steady course presenting him with an easy attack problem. Of the four torpedoes fired from his stern tubes, two hit the leading freighter and one struck the other ship on her quarter.

The first ship was brought to a standstill and was soon obviously sinking, but the other was still moving slowly and steering boldly for the periscope of the *Wahoo* which was turning to bring her bow tubes to bear. At this moment a third ship, previously hidden behind the others, was sighted coming foolishly along on the same course to take two torpedoes squarely in her hull. O'Kane swung the periscope on to the second freighter. Her captain certainly did not lack resolution. Crippled as she was, she was still coming on, slowly and ponderously, and by now her bow, which could crush the submarine's conning tower like an eggshell, was quite close. Morton gave the order for two torpedoes to be fired 'down the throat' before going deep. O'Kane had time to see one hit before the periscope dipped; but still the indomitable merchantman came on and only failed by a narrow margin to ram the *Wahoo*.

While the submarine stayed deep to reload her tubes, explosions rumbled round her, whether from depth-charges or the bursting boilers of the first freighter which took her final plunge at this time was never known. Eight minutes later the *Wahoo* was at periscope depth again, surveying the scene. Two ships were still on the surface, the crippled freighter still under way and now steering away and the third ship stopped, her character revealed by the swarm of Japanese soldiers on deck. Morton decided to finish her off and, with the troopship firing every one of her numerous guns at the periscope, he moved relentlessly in to the kill. His first torpedo ran deep and passed harmlessly underneath, but his second struck squarely amidships. The ship began to settle and as she went down the soldiers were seen 'jumping over the sides like ants off a hot plate!'

Morton now set off after the crippled freighter. Incredibly, twice torpedoed, she was still making six knots. The *Wahoo*'s battery was by now getting low. She could not afford the submerged speed to catch the fugitive. Just as Morton was deciding to take up the chase on the surface, yet another ship hove in sight which turned out to be a tanker, always a high priority target. It seemed that one or the other of the enemy would have to be allowed to escape; but the tanker now most conveniently turned to join up with the cripple. Exultantly Morton surfaced and began an 'end-around' to get ahead while charging his batteries at the same time.

It was not until 5.30 p.m., with sunset half an hour away, that he was ahead in position to dive. Both targets were keeping up a wide zigzag making a difficult attack problem, but an hour later Morton had got his boat to within 2000 yards of the tanker. One of the three bow torpedoes fired scored a hit. It was not enough to stop a tanker and in the growing darkness the *Wahoo* surfaced. All her bow torpedoes had now been expended and Morton was faced with the tricky problem of getting lined up for a stern shot on a widely zigzagging target. For an hour and a half his every effort was frustrated. Once he tried approaching stern first only to find that his rudder was forced hard over to one side against the influence of the steering engine, putting the boat out of control.

In the meantime, however, the tanker's zigzagging pattern had been studied and it became clear that each alteration of course was one of ninety degrees. Morton was thus able to anticipate her movements and to place himself so that the *Wahoo* was running parallel to the target at 1850 yards on one leg of the zigzag. So stationed he was able to swing round to present his tail at the tanker and fire two stern torpedoes. One hit amidships, breaking the tanker's back.

With only two stern torpedoes remaining, the *Wahoo* now set off after the crippled freighter. The same problem presented itself, increased by the fighting spirit of the freighter's crew who now, in spite of the darkness, opened a hot and accurate fire on the surfaced submarine. Shell splashes crept closer and closer until the risk of a disabling hit forced Morton to give the order to dive for a while before surfacing again to resume the chase. The target's irregular zigzag brought it continued immunity. That and her gun crews' good shooting might have saved her. But suddenly, on the far horizon, a searchlight beam flashed. Belatedly the Japanese were sending succour to their transports. The freighter headed for the hoped-for protection.

It was a fatal move. For now Morton could anticipate the target's course. He steered away for a position ahead of it and there lay in wait. The freighter was almost within sight of her rescuer when the *Wahoo*'s last two torpedoes struck a finally fatal blow. The Japanese crew perhaps deserved a better reward for their dogged defence. Mush Morton was too much of a realist to lavish sympathy on them as he composed the signal reporting his achievement: 'In ten-hour running gun and torpedo battle destroyed entire convoy of two freighters, one transport, one tanker. All torpedoes expended. Returning home.'

This would have satisfied most submariners, who would have allowed nothing to deflect them from their course for base, which in the *Wahoo*'s case meant the rare comforts of Pearl Harbor on this occasion. Not so the irrepressible Morton. At the sight of a convoy of three, apparently unescorted, he decided to try to sink one of them by gunfire, a small tanker straggling somewhere behind the remainder. He had barely surfaced when out of a rainsquall emerged an escort. As the water around erupted in shell splashes the raucous note of the klaxon brayed the order for a crash dive.

The *Wahoo* was well down before the first depth-charges exploded and they did little harm. Morton had nearly burnt his fingers; but that this had upset his good humour in any way was disproved by the signal which went on the air to base as soon as he was able to surface again: 'Another running gunfight. Destroyer gunning. *Wahoo* running!'

There was no disagreement at Hawaii with the *Wahoo*'s right to flaunt a broom at her masthead on entering harbour to signify a clean sweep, as the famous old Dutchman Van Tromp is said to have done.

The *Wahoo*'s next patrol was to the Yellow Sea, waters which at that time – the spring of 1943 – had not before been a hunting ground for submarines. Morton made the most of the advantage of surprise and in a period of ten days in March sank eight freighters and a troop transport. By August 1943 Mush Morton and the *Wahoo* were a combination which seemed unbeatable and they set out on their sixth patrol from Pearl Harbor refreshed by a refit in an American port and full of confidence. Inevitably there had been many changes in the crew as officers and men were drafted away to man newly built submarines. Dick O'Kane had left to take command of the *Tang*. George Grider was another, promoted first to be executive officer of the *Pollack* and later to command the *Flasher*. It is not without significance that both of these who had served their apprenticeship with Morton were to prove outstanding fighting submariners. Meanwhile there can be no doubt that Morton must have missed the companionship of O'Kane, the other half of the perfect attack team they made in combination.

And now there came signs that the *Wahoo*'s luck was running out fast. For this sixth patrol she was ordered to the Sea of Japan, the waters between Japan and the mainland. They were waters perilous on account of numerous minefields and anti-submarine forces, surface and air. But the rewards were expected to be large as a great many ships passed through the area. Morton waded into them with all his customary gusto. In four days he attacked nine fat freighters – but not one of them did he sink. Every one of the ten torpedoes he fired failed to function correctly, either breaking surface, running at the wrong depth or on erratic courses or simply failing to detonate. Morton's hitherto unfailing good temper and cool confidence were for once broken down. He and his men were risking their lives for nothing. Reporting the circumstances he was recalled to Pearl Harbor.

There the remainder of his torpedoes were discarded and a full load of the new Mark 18 electric torpedoes taken on board. Morton asked to be allowed to return to the same waters for the next patrol. On 20 September the *Wahoo* passed through the La Pérouse Strait between Japan and Sakhalin. Thereafter nothing more was heard from her. As the silence lengthened beyond the date set for her to leave the Sea of Japan at the end of her patrol, anxiety for her fate grew finally into a sad acceptance of her loss. On 9 November it was officially reported that Mush Morton and the *Wahoo* would never again enter harbour, the broom at the masthead. Only after the war could evidence be pieced together to discover the facts. Four Japanese ships had been sunk by the *Wahoo*, one of them a large troopship with more than five hundred troops on board. On 11 October 1943 a Japanese anti-submarine aircraft surprised a submarine on the surface in the La Pérouse Strait. This was almost certainly the *Wahoo*. Three depth-charges fell round her as she was submerging. What happened then is guesswork. Perhaps her pressure hull was ruptured. Perhaps she was thrown out of control to plane down below her safe depth to be crushed by the immense water pressure deep down. Whatever it was, one of the great heroes of the war had gone.

9 Midgets attack giants

Godfrey Place

X-craft were midget submarines fifteen metres long, weighing thirty-five tonnes, capable of making six and a half knots on the surface, five knots submerged, and of diving to 900 metres depth. They were manned by three officers and one engine-room artificer, who were highly trained, and could live for ten to fourteen days in their appallingly cramped conditions while travelling 2400 kilometres. Their only weapons were two two-tonne explosives which they dropped on the sea bed underneath their targets and which were fired by clockwork time-fuses. X-craft were intended for use against ships and installations strongly defended in harbours or other anchorages.

In 1943 one of the targets assigned to the midgets were the huge German battleships *Tirpitz*, *Scharnhorst* and *Lutzow* then lying in Norwegian fjords safe from attack by air or sea and waiting for a chance to prey on Allied shipping.

It was vital that these impressive warships be put out of action. Six X-craft were sent to destroy them. X5, X6 and X7 were sent against *Tirpitz*, X9 and X10 against *Scharnhorst* and X8 against *Lutzow*.

X7's captain, Godfrey Place VC, DSC, VM (the Polish VC), RN, describes the attack on *Tirpitz*, giving a vivid picture of midget submarine warfare methods.

On the evening of the 18th, although the weather left much to be desired, we decided to change crews. The actual change-over was satisfactory, but when *Stubborn* got under way again it seemed to me, on the casing of X7, that the tow was extremely long – it was, it had parted again. We only had two rope tows with us, so we were forced to use the last resort, a two and a half inch wire. It was no joke securing this in the sea conditions that prevailed, and Bill Whittam and I – secured by lines to the boat against being washed overboard – spent three exhausting hours on the casing before X7 was finally in tow again. We were neither of us dry nor in good humour when we went below, but the orderliness within was a delight to be seen. One would hardly have known that three men had spent a week in this confined space, and the mechanical efficiency of the machinery was in keeping – the passage crew could not have done their job better.

The next day was a lazy one – on these occasions the human being seems to develop an almost infinite capacity for sleep, uncomfortable as his bed may be.

The only excitement before we slipped was Minerva. By that night, the 19th, we were within twenty miles of the slipping position and the weather had cleared completely. X7 was on the surface and charging to full capacity. Bill Whittam was keeping a lookout through the night periscope and the rest of us were having supper.

'*Stubborn*'s flashing and there is something bumping up against the bow,' he announced. I looked through the periscope. There was something bumping against the bow, but I couldn't make out what.

'I'll go and have a look,' I said, and Bill went back to the periscope.

'You'd better hurry – it's a mine.'

I did. It was a German one, whose broken mooring had half hitched itself round the tow and come to rest against X7's bow. I noticed it was painted green and black, that it was obviously freshly laid and that one horn had already been broken, but I didn't wait to examine it closely; keeping it off with my foot gingerly placed on its shell I loosed its mooring wire from the tow and breathed more deeply as it floated astern. When I got below I thought a tot wouldn't do us any harm, so we toasted the Geneva Convention and Minerva – the mine with the crumpled horn.

The night of the 20th was beautifully calm with only a gentle swell from the west. We slipped at 20.00, exchanged a few comments on this and that with *Stubborn* and set a course for Stjernsund. During the night we saw one other X-craft, I think X5, but otherwise nothing. The internal exhaust pipe from the engine split just before dawn, so the fumes had to be extracted by the air compressor and X7 dived, rather later than had been intended, at 01.45. At 02.30 we came up to periscope depth and were able to identify the entrance to Stjernsund. (Times in this narrative are GMT – the sun rising at about 02.00 and setting at 19.00.)

The day, calm and peaceful, was spent mostly at ninety feet, coming to periscope depth to fix our position every hour or so. In Stjernsund the water was like a sheet of turquoise stained glass, the steep sides of the fjord luxurious in browns and greens emphasised by the bright sunlight and the Norwegian fishing boats, picturesque enough for even the most blasé traveller. There were occasional patches of snow on the higher ground, but the water – clear as a mountain stream – did not appear to be very cold.

At 12.30 we entered Altenfjord proper, where there was sufficient lop on the surface to allow us to raise the induction trunk and release the excess of pressure within the boat that five hours with the oxygen switched on had caused.

At 19.45 we surfaced, and Whitley immediately started to fit the spare for the broken section of the exhaust pipe – regrettably without success; however, canvas bandages and spun yarn made the fracture reasonably gas-tight and the charge was started about an hour after surfacing. The boat was cleaned up generally and empty tins, used protosorb and the used oxygen bottles were thrown overboard. Rafsbotm itself was the anchorage for German fleet auxiliaries, so the charge and the tidying up had to be stopped for short periods from time to time when small craft appeared to be heading our way and it was thought wiser to dive out of sight, but the weather was in our favour – overcast and enough wind to cover the noise of our engine. Not long after the charge had been started, searchlights and starshell were seen to the northward, near the top of Altenfjord – at first it was feared that an X-craft had been located, but it was probably the *Scharnhorst* on night exercises. (She had been sighted anchored south of Arnoy Island when we went by that afternoon: a sitting target, but we were after larger fish.)

At 01.00 on the 22nd the charge was stopped, the few engine fumes that had escaped extracted by the compressor, and X7 dived to make her way for the entrance of Kafjord.

Before 04.00 the gap in the anti-submarine nets at the entrance had been located (it was over a hundred yards wide and had no way of shutting it) but we waited for a minesweeper to come out before entering – her ensign was the first I had seen worn by an enemy ship in commission. To avoid any close watch there might be at the entrance (the day was calm and clear with only a slight surface ruffle) X7 entered at forty feet, but on coming to periscope depth inside had to be taken down again immediately to avoid a small motorboat. Somewhat uncertain of our position relative to the ships and net defences inside, X7 was brought up again as soon as seemed reasonable, but at thirty feet the boat ran into an anti-torpedo net – the water was clear enough to see it and it appeared as the most formidable-looking underwater defence I had seen. The wire of which it was constructed was thin, not more than an inch in circumference, but was meshed into squares less than six inches across and there seemed to be at least two such thicknesses, presenting a baffling jazz pattern to the observer. X7 was stuck, she did not 'fall out' when the motor was stopped, nor when slow astern speeds were tried. (High speeds were considered unwise lest the disturbance of the buoys on the surface betray our presence.) The internal tanks were flooded in the hope that the boat would 'fall out' with the increased weight but this had no effect and the pump was run to get back to normal trim. After ten minutes it was apparent that this pump was not sucking out any water. We tried the other pump, with almost laughable results — there was a single spark from the commutator casing of its motor but otherwise no movement. No. 2 main ballast was blown right out but X7 did not float out of the net. Finally, all main ballast tanks were blown, and the main motor run for two minutes full ahead and then put full astern, so that X7 could gather as much way as the slack in the nets would allow. She came clear — all main ballast tanks were vented but the boat did break surface before going to the bottom like a stone, more than half a ton heavy. We thought this escapade would be certain to invoke some attention even if we ourselves had not been seen. I felt they could not fail to notice the bubbles from the vented main ballast tanks.

We waited on the bottom for about twenty minutes to give the gyro a chance to steady (we had already been an hour in the net) then blew No. 2 main ballast tank gently — when it was right we still had not left the bottom and I noticed that a large wire (presumably a wire securing the nets we had recently been in) was across our periscope standard. However, a burst of full speed and a little air in 1 and 3 was enough to clear us, and we immediately left that unpleasant spot.

Trimming by air was not easy in these craft, but without pumps there was no choice. When we left the bottom this time we did, admittedly, break surface for a second or two, but subsequently Whittam managed it perfectly, using Q and 2 MB for bodily weight, and moving Aitken (who, unfortunate individual, had no job during an attack).

At 06.40, when X7 was close to the northward of a tanker of the *Altmark* class, the *Tirpitz* was sighted for the first time at a range of about a mile.

My intention for the attack was to go deep at a range of 500 yards, pass under the anti-torpedo nets at seventy feet and run down the length of the target from bow to stern, letting go one charge under the bridge, the other well aft and altering to port to escape under the nets on the *Tirpitz*'s starboard side.

At 07.05 X7 was taken to seventy feet for the attack but stuck in the net instead of passing underneath. This time I had no intention of staying there. By similar tactics to those that extricated us before, but without breaking surface, we came out and tried again at ninety feet, this time getting more firmly stuck. On occasions when the craft is being navigated blind, it is extremely difficult to know one's position to within a hundred yards – in this case the *Tirpitz*, the nets and the shore were all within a circle of that diameter, and the gyro had again gone off the board with the excessive angles the boat had taken. Thus when X7 next came clear and started rising, the motor was stopped lest she run up the beach or on to the top of the nets and fall into enemy hands. When she broke surface I saw we were inside the close-net defences (how we got underneath I have no idea) about thirty yards from the *Tirpitz*'s port beam – 'group up, full ahead, forty feet'.

We actually hit the target's side obliquely at twenty feet and slid underneath, swinging our fore-and-aft line to the line of her keel. The first charge was let go – as I estimated under the *Tirpitz*'s bridge – and X7 was taken about 200 feet astern to drop the other charge under the after turrets. The time was 07.20. It was just as we were letting go the second charge that we heard the first signs of enemy counter-attack – but, oddly enough, we were wrong in assuming they were meant for us.

In X7 we had to guess a course that we hoped would take us back to that lucky spot where we had got under the nets on our way in; but we were not lucky. We tried in many places within a few feet of the bottom, but in vain, and rapidly lost all sense of our exact position. The gyro was still chasing its tail and the magnetic compass could not be raised for fear it would foul some wire or a portion of a net; we did use the course indicator (a form of compass that remains steady during alterations of course but does indicate true position) but the noise it made was most tiresome so we switched it off again.

The next three-quarters of an hour were very trying; exactly what track X7 made I have no idea, but we tried most places along the bottom of those nets, passing under the *Tirpitz* again more than once, and even breaking surface at times, but nowhere could we find a way out. We had to blow each time we got into the nets and the HP air was getting down to a dangerously low level – but bull-in-a-china-shop tactics were essential as our charges had been set with only an hour's delay – and those of others might go up at any time after eight o'clock. The small charges that were periodically dropped by the Germans were not likely to do us any harm and, when we were on the surface, no guns larger than light automatic weapons which caused no damage could be brought to bear – but we were sceptical about our chances against at least four tons of torpex exploding within a hundred yards. But the luck that had recently deserted us came back for a few minutes shortly after eight.

We came to the surface – an original method, but we were halfway across before I realised what was happening. On the other side we dived to the bottom and at once started to get under way again to put as much distance as possible between us and the coming explosion. Sticking again in a net at sixty feet was the limit, as this confounded my estimate of our position relative to the nets. But we were not here long before the explosion came – a continuous roar that seemed to last whole minutes. The damage it caused X7 was really surprisingly small – depth-gauges, trimming bubble and some lights broken; considerable but not catastrophic leaks at most hull glands; the gyro spinning with almost the speed of its rotor – but the hull was still complete.

An incidental effect of the explosion was to shake us out of the net, so we sat at the bottom to review our position. We had no pumps that would work; the HP air bottles were empty, but internal venting where possible had increased the air pressure within the boat and the compressor was still working. The leaks were not immediately dangerous, but, as we had no way of pumping them out, we could not afford to delay. So we set off again, aiming at taking advantage of the confusion to get a good check on our position (I was not really certain we were even out of the nets) and then lying up and refitting on the bottom in shallow water.

Nos. 1 and 3 MB tanks had to be blown to get us off bottom and with air in these open-bottom tanks, depth-keeping was impossible – we could choose only between surface and bottom. Nor was I correct in thinking we would be able to fix our position when we were on the surface (it was provoking to see the *Tirpitz* still on the surface, but that was about all that could be seen). We did another of these hops to the surface and this time the night periscope was hit; as it was probable we had only enough air for one more surface and there was no chance of getting away, we decided to abandon ship. DSEA escape was considered, but we were not keen to risk depth-charges that were being dropped, so it was decided to try a surface surrender first. If firing did not stop at the showing of a white sweater, we could always try DSEA from the bottom after a delay to allow enemy activity to die down.

X7 was surfaced and I, gingerly, I must confess, opened the fore hatch just enough to allow the waving of a white sweater. Firing did immediately stop, so I came outside and waved the sweater more vigorously.

The Germans had put a battle-practice target some 500 yards off the starboard bow of the *Tirpitz* – probably an attempt to obscure other attacking craft's view of their target – and X7 hit this just after I came on the casing, with her extremely low bouyancy forward – one main ballast tank had presumably been hit – the curved side of this was sufficient to force the bow down so that water went into the wet-and-dry before I could shut the hatch. From Aitken's description this was probably not more than thirty gallons, but it was sufficient to send X7 to the bottom again – I was left on the battle-practice target.

From Aitken's description of subsequent events inside X7 it is clear that Whittam managed everything with great calm and skill. A DSEA escape was planned and a certain amount of wrecking of more secret machinery carried out. They waited more than an hour and then decided to make their escape. From this depth – 120 feet – the oxygen in a DSEA set lasts very little time, so it is imperative that the boat is flooded as quickly as possible until the pressure within is the same as that outside and the hatches can be opened; also those escaping must breathe the air in the boat until the batteries are flooded and the air foul with gas. In this case the drill was perfect, but only one small hull valve could be opened for the flooding up – all others were tried and why they had jammed is impossible to say – perhaps the explosion was the cause. Thus it was that only Aitken managed to conserve his oxygen long enough for a successful escape – he gave the other two their emergency supply when they had already lost consciousness but they did not revive, and Aitken himself was picked up on the surface in a comatose condition.

I can only voice my disappointment that all my crew were not successful at this last hazard. When X7 went down I thought they would be, but perhaps we had already had more than our fair share of naturals. Whittam – six foot five of English public school with stories as tall as himself; Whitley – older than any of us, a gay lad whose father was waiting for him to take over his engineering works in the Midlands.

For my own part I felt ridiculous walking on to the quarterdeck of a Fleet flagship wearing vest, pants, sea-boot stockings and army boots size twelve. When I was told that I would be shot if I did not state where I had laid my mines (this much, at least, they now knew by surmise) I stated I was an English naval officer and as such demanded the courtesy entitled to my rank. (I didn't say what rank – I had a fleeting vision of Gabby, the town crier in Max Fleischer's cartoon of *Gulliver's Travels*, shouting, 'You can't do this to me, you can't do this to me – I've a wife and kids, millions of kids.')

10 The 'Scharnhorst' has been sunk!

B. B. Ramsden

Scharnhorst survived the midget submarine attack, but her fate was sealed. She could not be allowed to raid on Allied shipping unchecked. And at last the chance the British navy had been waiting for came on Boxing Day, 26 December 1943. That day the mighty *Scharnhorst* met her rival, the Royal Navy battleship *Duke of York*. After a carefully managed chase involving the RN cruisers *Onslow, Belfast, Sheffield, Norfolk, Jamaica* and four destroyers, *Duke of York* got in range of the quarry. The first rounds were fired at 4.50 p.m.

This was to be the last great sea battle between huge capital ships without help from the air, a slogging match between giants, and an historic encounter.

Lieutenant B. B. Ramsden, a Royal Marines officer aboard HMS *Jamaica*, described the action, 'The Sinking of the Scharnhorst', in *Blackwood's Magazine* for November 1944. Before the German ship was finally beaten she sustained hits by thirteen 14-inch shells, at least twelve 8-inch shells and eleven torpedo explosions. Only thirty-six of her total 2000 crew survived.

The first shot was fired in starshell by the *Duke of York*'s 5.25-inch turrets, and the report sounded dull and metallic to us. I raised my head from the binoculars and counted the seconds till one and then another burst into flickering light over the horizon. At first we could see nothing until one or two burst over to the right of the others, and suddenly – there she was! A vague illuminated silhouette – the *Scharnhorst*. Almost as soon as she could be seen, there was a deafening crack and a spurt of flame as we fired our first full broadside of six-inch. The concussion momentarily deafened me, and my vision was blurred by the shaking of the director and the sudden flash out of the gloom. We could see the tracer shells coursing away like a swarm of bees bunched together, and could follow them as they curved gently down towards the target. Before they landed, the guns spoke again, and the sea was lighted for a brief second by the livid flash.

Then the *Duke of York* fired her fourteen-inch, and even to us, now a thousand yards astern, the noise and concussion was colossal, and the vivid spurt of flame lighted up the whole ship for an instant, leaving a great drift of cordite smoke hanging in the air. Her tracers rose quickly and, in a bunch, sailed up to the highest point of their trajectory, and then curved down, down towards the target.

I think we had fired two or three broadsides before the reply came. Her first retaliation was by starshell, probably from her 5.9s using relatively flashless cordite, as we did. From that distance the firing of these was quite invisible until the shells burst, two or three together, with intense white flares which hung in the air above us. In their light the sea was lit up as by the moon very brightly, and I remember thinking that we must have been visible for miles. I felt as if I had been stripped stark naked, and had to resist the natural urge to hide behind something away from the light, as if it would have mattered! After what seemed like an age her starshell dimmed and guttered out in a shower of bright sparks, which fell down to the sea for all the world like stubbing out a pipe at night. Just as we had again been plunged into the comforting gloom I saw the angry white wink of her first eleven-inch broadside, and said half down the telephone and half to myself, 'She's fired' – not very comforting to those below, and not much better for me. Thank God we couldn't see her shells coming as we could see ours going. The waiting for their arrival was bad enough, but to see them coming all the way would have been far more grim. There was a vague flash off the port bow which I caught in the corner of my eye as I gazed through the binoculars, and then – crack, crack, crack, sharp like a giant whip, and the drone and whine of splinters passing somewhere near.

I don't know how much I was scared then – quite enough, anyway, though there was too much happening really to be properly frightened. The whizz of the shell splinters was the nastiest of all, as the director, with open face, was trained directly towards the enemy, and the clearance of my head above the binocular sight assumed, mentally, abnormal proportions. The trouble was, seated rigidly and surrounded by instruments and voice-pipe, I could only move enough to save one portion of my anatomy from temporary paralysis, to the subsequent detriment of another, even under normal cruising conditions, and now I felt an extreme urge for comforting protection!

Almost as soon as the first shells burst, the CP called up – 'Some shells landed pretty near us then, didn't they, sir? We felt 'em down here very plainly.' At that, any personal thought or introspection vanished from me, and I realised that it was up to me to say something comforting even to the point of obscuring the truth from those below who could neither see nor imagine much of what was happening. I replied in as much of a matter-of-fact voice as was available that I believed something had arrived somewhere near, but I wasn't very sure. These were the first proper words I had spoken since the action was joined, and it was personally reassuring to hear myself say something coolly and in a detached manner. Any further conversation was cut short by another six-inch broadside, and a few seconds later the same angry white wink on the horizon. This time I looked up and saw her shells burst for the first time, and in their light the splashes mast-high, and unpleasantly near the *Duke of York*, who was steadily crashing away with her full broadsides. Vaguely I heard my communication number, crouched down on a seat, beside me, saying, 'All right, Geordie. All right, Geordie,' to his opposite number in the ADP*. The *Scharnhorst* was retiring, and we were increasing speed to twenty-eight knots, with a slight turn to port as we made off in pursuit behind the flagship.

* Air Defence Platform.

For a short time no shot was fired, and I looked down to the for'ard turrets as they trained in unison, the guns in serried ranks raised threateningly, ready to fire again. We kept the director trained towards the enemy, altering the bearing against a change of course, and every minute or so the range was passed up to me, which I repeated for the benefit of the crew. It was steadily increasing. The flash and concussion of another broadside shook us again, but it no longer worried me. In fact it became rather a thrill eventually, and its power gave me a subtle exhilaration from a sense of our might, although there still remained in the back of my mind the knowledge that the flash gave away our range and position to the *Scharnhorst* every time we fired. After a little the range increased, which rendered our six-inch rather out of it, and that, combined with the fact that our shell-splashes might have confused the flagship's spotting, made us cease fire temporarily, and we could follow the battle more closely. It was a slogging match between giants, appalling in their might and fury. Every time the *Duke of York* fired there came the vivid flicker of the *Scharnhorst*'s reply, the lazy flight of the fourteen-inch tracer, followed by the crack, crack of the eleven-inch reply in the sea, and the drone of splinters.

At one period we were engaging her fire off our starboard bow, and both sides fired a succession of starshell for the greater accuracy of their main armaments. I suddenly remembered my camera, and withdrew my gloves to fish it out of my oilskins. My fingers were wet and cold, and I fumbled wildly. Leaning to one side for a clearer view, I sighted it nicely just as about six starshells were in the air, and took a long shot. As I released the catch to finish, A and B turrets fired again, and I whipped it up once more in an attempt to catch the tracers before they became too vague in the distance.

Suddenly the ship was bathed in light again as starshell flared directly overhead, and simultaneously liquid deluged down over the director and streamed over my face. For a second there passed through my mind that it had come from a bursting shell – or some filthy chemical which might burn or disfigure. I passed my tongue over my lips and tasted the stuff. It had a queer tang. God – could it be ..? and just as quickly it surged to my mind that it was no more harmful than plain salt sea water! As I discovered some hours after the action, an eleven-inch shell had landed in the water starboard side and abreast of B turret, only half the ship's breadth from our side. It sent up a column of water, which then collapsed all over the bridge and decks, and had, of course, drowned us as well.

Still the slogging match continued, flash for flash, round for round. Although the *Scharnhorst* was not firing at us directly, the shells were falling sometimes to miss the flagship and to come uncomfortably close to us. At one moment I thought the *Duke of York* was hit. Simultaneously with the burst of three eleven-inch close to her, a red glow blossomed from somewhere for'ard and lit up her entire bridge superstructure. However, it turned out to be the flash of her reply from A turret, which was suffused in the billowing cordite smoke. This drifted back in acrid clouds, and was most unpleasant. We turned a few points to starboard at high speed, and I could again train the director on to the *Scharnhorst*'s flickering salvos. I tried to give a running commentary over the telephone to those below, but it must have been most disjointed.

'Boxing Day, bulletin number 30.' Again the cheerful voice of the first lieutenant. 'The destroyers are now going in to attack.' I confess to having completely forgotten about them up till then, but now I blessed their presence. There was a strange lull in the gunfire. Everyone was on tiptoe, straining to catch the first signs of their attack. The familiar flash of eleven-inch again split the darkness, and a minute or so later an incredible and terrifying noise made me momentarily crouch down again. A whole salvo had passed clean over our heads, like the tearing of a huge corrugated cardboard box – an indescribable devilish sound. 'Come on, Adolf, no more of that,' I prayed. Again the flicker in the distance, and again we waited for it to arrive. Nothing came. Again the flash, but followed this time by starshell illuminating the horizon. Thank God, the destroyers must be in. We remained silent and sat back more comfortably.

Then the flagship turned, slowly at first, to port, and round we went farther and farther in her faint wake until our bows were directly towards the enemy. They were getting excited below. Dead ahead were the signs of a furious engagement. Starshell flared high, guns flashed, red beads of pompom fire ran out in livid streams, each to fade in a small white burst. Strange bursts of high-angle fire spasmodically dotted the sky, and still we ploughed on steadily and silently, and our guns pointed mutely towards the flashes ready to crash out again.

No shell came near us for almost twenty minutes. We turned to starboard, the turrets following round so that both ships presented a full broadside. I think I yelled 'Stand by again!' over the telephones, but my words were drowned by the deafening crash of gunfire. The tracer now appeared almost horizontal, so flat was the trajectory as they rushed like fireflies to converge at a point in the darkness.

Suddenly—a bright-red glow, and in it the enemy was to be clearly seen for a brief moment. 'She's hit! My God, we've got her!' I was yelling like one possessed. We were cheering in the director. All over the ship a cheer went up, audible above the gunfire. I had risen half standing in my seat as the wild thrill took hold of me. Again the dull glow, and in its light the sea was alive with shell-splashes from an outpouring of shells. Great columns of water stood out clearly in the brief instant of light, and I could see smoke hanging above her. I was mad with excitement until I realised that my ravings must be an incoherent babble of enthusiasm to those below as the telephones were still hanging round my head. I straightened my tin hat, sat down, and told them as calmly as I could that we could see that our shells had set her on fire, and that both the *Duke of York* and ourselves were hitting, and hitting hard.

She must have been a hell on earth. The fourteen-inch from the flagship were hitting or rocketing off from a ricochet on the sea. I had no coherent thought. The sudden knowledge that we were beating her to a standstill had gone to my head. My crew were just as bad. Nothing seemed to matter. Great flashes rent the night, and the sound of gunfire was continuous, and yet the *Scharnhorst* replied, but only occasionally now. She was engaging the destroyers with what armament she had.

We were keeping the director trained dead on her, and none of us noticed that our course had altered. The blaze and concussion of our gunfire seemed to grow, and, as in a dream, I heard someone shout, 'The back of the director's blown in, sir.' A second later something hit me in the back, and lay there heavy and inanimate. I looked round and saw that indeed it had been blown in. The hinges had given under the blast of our turrets, and left a gaping rectangular space through which the wind and spray whistled. It occurred to me quickly that another broadside would go off any moment, and the flash come in on our unprotected backs, and so we trained on to the beam just in time. The next broadside left us dazed, but what did we care! I crawled out of my seat and crouched at the side, gripping on to a strut to steady myself for the next. A and B turrets were trained until the muzzle gave our director a minimum of clearance, and the shells could be passing only a few feet away from us. We clung to anything, and gazed intent on the target as the blast and flash of our broadside shook the director like a can. It was terrific.

Then faintly, but growing more loud and clear as we ceased firing, came the pipe – 'Boxing Day, bulletin number 38. Commander-in-Chief ordered *Jamaica* to go in and finish her off with torpedoes.' A moment later, divorced at last from the comfort of the flagship's heavy guns, we turned, in a sweep of spray, bows on again towards where we had last seen the *Scharnhorst*'s flash. We were alone.

How alone we felt! The tumult and the noise had died,

leaving almost a hush – the hush of expectancy. All I could hear was the wind and the sea, and into the quiet came the return of foreboding and tension. Everyone was thinking – what lies ahead? When last seen, the *Scharnhorst* was still firing. Had she any eleven-inch yet able to bear on us? As we closed what sudden crash of gunfire might envelop us? God, how much nearer? A sudden large flash ahead. Wait!— no, nothing arrived near us. Still firing at the destroyers, perhaps. 'Stand by, four-inch, port side,' came the order down a voice-pipe.

I was galvanised into action. 'Train round, train round. Stop. No, a little more. There she is! Guns follow director. Enemy in sight. No deflection. You've got the range, haven't you? OK. Stand by, then.' It had come. At last we were going to open fire, and I was controlling. I was cool now, and desperately grim in concentration. I mustn't lose this chance. We were turning, turning to starboard, and again came the flicker of gunfire right in front of us, but much more vivid and far nearer. I caught sight of a red blob, then another, which rose in front and then curved down, and it seemed to come straight for us. No, it had gone over. Again everything blurred, and was shaken as one six-inch broadside and then another was fired – straight into her. We couldn't miss at that range – 3000 yards. I could smell the sweetish smell of burning. It must be the *Scharnhorst*. I yelled above the din for permission to open fire. We waited and waited for an answer, but none came. They probably never received it on the bridge. And then we turned away and ceased firing. My four-inch hadn't even opened up, and we were bitterly disappointed.

Starshell from nowhere burst over our heads, bathing the whole ship in light. Surely she will open up now. We were naked, illuminated in every detail. But nothing came. No shot was fired at us, and once more everything was plunged in darkness. At 3500 yards we turned a full half-circle, so that our starboard side was presented, and we on the port side could sit back and try to imagine what was happening. Another burst of fire and more flashes. Then we turned away and made off. There was no noise now. What had happened? Nobody seemed to know. What had become of the torpedoes? As I was trying to find out from the ADP, two distinct underwater explosions, deep and dull, made the ship quiver slightly. 'Those were our "fish" hitting!' came the cry. Still there was no noise of firing. We stood up in the director and looked around. Nothing in sight. Ten minutes passed and nothing happened. Hardly a sound could be heard above the wind and the sea. We asked the ADP if they could see anything, and they told us that there was one solitary searchlight burning on the starboard side, sweeping the sea, over which could be seen a vague pall of smoke. Minutes dragged by. What was happening? Where was everyone?

'Boxing Day, bulletin number 43,' came the pipe, and, in scarcely suppressed excitement, 'The *Scharnhorst* has been sunk. Destroyers are picking up survivors.'

11 D-Day

William Pugsley and Denis Glover

The Royal Navy's role in the invasion of Europe by Allied forces was without equal in history. A vast army and all its equipment, including an enormous prefabricated harbour, had to be shipped across the treacherous waters of the English Channel and be put ashore on the most heavily defended coastline ever encountered. But it was achieved, this amazing feat of co-operation, planning and military administration.

William H. Pugsley of the Royal Canadian Navy was in the minesweeper fleet that day and described his part in the action in *Saints, Devils and Ordinary Seamen*. The sweepers went ahead of the main force to clear the sea of mines, making a carefully thought-out path for the armada.

By sundown our little flotilla of sweepers was hurrying south-east for the rendezvous from which the whole invasion fleet would head for France. From far away downwind on our port side came the steady drone of hundreds and hundreds of landing craft heading in the same direction, white water flashing from their blunt bows in the last of the daylight.

That night we fixed bayonets on the ship's rifles.

We were perhaps a little disturbed as we sailed towards Normandy. Only a fool wouldn't be. We'd be right out in front, sweeping a path for the armada that followed. With the dragging weight of a sweep out astern, our manoeuvrability would be almost nil. Thus would we meet the Luftwaffe, out in force to protect the Atlantic West Wall, since surely the easiest time to stop us would be before we got a footing on the land.

No one spoke about it, but every one of us expected

bombs, torpedoes, gunfire, mines, E-boats, destroyers, secret weapons of new and horrible types, and gas. Besides our ordinary respirators we were issued with transparent visors against liquid gas. Each was good for only fifteen minutes. Then you tore it off and put on a fresh one – very quickly.

Fellows went about quietly making their own arrangements for the coming fray. Silently they adjusted the bands of their tin hats, checked their identification tags, made sure their life-jacket flashlight worked, and tied their most precious possessions in a small bag at the waist. One lad was practically draped in razor-sharp sheath knives. 'Figurin' on some hand-to-hand fightin'?' I asked. 'You never know,' he answered vaguely.

The boys were very keen on the new RCN life-jackets. We were practically living in them now. They'd been issued on board the 'Tribal' destroyer *Athabaskan* just before she went out on her last patrol, and they saved many lives then. We liked them and were preparing to float around in them indefinitely as survivors.

Choice edibles the fellows had been hoarding in their lockers now came to light. Nothing could have shown more clearly what they thought was ahead than the way in which they now brought out these tidbits from home and insisted that we eat them – right away, while we still could! No use going into the water on an empty stomach! Even the canteen manager began to have doubts, and let us buy all the chocolate bars we wanted. It was a regular Belshazzar's feast.

I'd never seen ratings taking things so seriously. They tested the escape hatch in the mess deck to see that it worked, and the ladder to be sure it came free easily. One of the 'Killicks' checked and double-checked the 'bottom line' that ran around the bow to take a collision mat in case we got holed. At night, without any orders whatsoever, guys went round checking up on the ship's blackout, so no chink of light showed to a prowling E-boat. I even went and hacked off my lovely beard, after reading in an old newspaper how bearded survivors from the torpedoed frigate *Valleyfield* nearly choked to death in fuel oil!

All next day there were vapour trails overhead from passing aircraft. They could be enemy planes just as easily as ours, for all we knew, and the lookouts were supposed to report each trail they saw. If a man off watch and passing the time of day on deck spotted one of these trails before the nearby lookout did, he gave his shipmate a terrific blast for not keeping his eyes open. 'I'm not going to swim just because of you,' he nattered.

We hadn't started our sweep yet, but it would be fairly simple. The ships, all twelve, would take up a sort of arrowhead formation. The leading ship would then put out a sweep on both sides, and the next ship behind her on each flank would put out a sweep in the direction of that flank. With each ship keeping her bow inside the end of the next ahead's sweep, we'd clear a wide channel and no one would hit anything. At least that was the theory!

Just in case anyone's wondering about it, I suppose I should add that there were two small Yankee MLs to sweep ahead of the flotilla and so protect the leading ship. The senior officer in the MLs, so we learned, was the man who'd spirited General MacArthur away from the Philippines.

Next morning we were having breakfast in the mess deck as usual. The sweep had been out since three o'clock, but everything was quiet, even the conversation. 'I've got my money and my liquor permit wrapped up in oiled silk. . . . What for? Your permit'll be no good in France. . . . I'll bet those Limies in the next sweeper will be out scrubbing down the fo'c'sle even with mines comin' up. . . . Pass the butter, you clown. . . . Get that life-jacket out of my way, will you, so a guy can drink his coffee? . . . Don't throw that tin away: I'm gonna use it for water to cool my Oerlikon barrel. . . . Wonder what kind of headlines this'll make back home? . . .' BOOM! BOOM!

The whole ship shook like a piece of sheet tin. There was a dead silence in the mess. Then it came again and much louder than before, BOOM! This time everything on the table leaped into the air. A voice yelled down through the for'ard hatchway: 'Hello, below! In case you're interested, we're cuttin' mines out here.' As if we didn't know!

Well, we rose from that table as one man. The first bloke took off with the coffee pot in one hand, his plate in the other, and his mouth so full of toast he couldn't speak. Another chap came flying out of the washroom in such a hurry he left his false teeth behind and had to go back for them. In about three seconds we were out of the mess deck, and had taken all the breakfast with us. We closed the door and dogged it down tight. That extra bulkhead would help a lot if we hit anything.

The last mine had blown the end off our sweep, and we were delayed getting a new one rigged. We didn't care much about the mines we cut, but those cut by the ship ahead might come up right in front of us. 'Now,' said the captain, 'all eyes ahead.' He needn't have worried: fully half the ship's company was watching intently already.

Oddly enough, no more mines were detonated that day. Several were cut by the ships ahead of us, and we tried to set them off by gunfire. They looked clean, as if they hadn't been down long. We opened up at them with all our small arms, but couldn't hit the horns. Then, as their outer casings became pierced with bullets, they filled and sank. One that popped up much too close for comfort had us pretty excited until it turned out to be an old bucket dropped overboard by HMCS *Vegreville* up ahead.

We were heading in straight for France now. Owing to bad weather in the Channel, there'd been a twenty-four hour postponement shortly after the start, but this didn't worry anyone except the cook. He had won the ship's five-pound sweep on the date of D-Day, and now he had to hand the money over to the leading writer.

As our flotilla swept a channel, trawlers put down spar buoys to mark the path. The buoys carried flags for daylight and dim blue-green lights for night. Far astern, but closing on us, we could now see a jumbled mass of invasion ships, their balloons mere black dots against the grey sky. On either side of them idled destroyers, PT boats, and cruisers.

By the middle of the afternoon one spearhead of the armada was right behind us. The landings were set to begin early the following morning. Besides the infantry and tank-carrying vessels, there were ocean-going tugs, landing craft towing barges laden with more landing craft, barges with heavy guns, and raft-like somethings barely awash with people walking about on them. There were also the rocket ships, looking like a direct steal from *Popular Science* or *Amazing Stories*.

In the early evening we were still roughly forty miles off the French coast. Everyone planned to spend the night on deck. The galley would make cocoa and sandwiches for us. The men were all much too curious to sleep when they came off watch. They were scared stiff they might miss something absolutely terrific.

We hadn't met any opposition at all so far. We couldn't understand it. Why hadn't there been any German planes? Lordy! Maybe they were waiting to trap us close in by the coast. We all knew what had happened off the shores of Greece and Crete.

But whatever the Germans did about the invasion fleet, obviously we'd catch it first, and the boys kept chattering contentedly about the awful time we'd be having in just a few hours. They weren't exactly measuring themselves mentally for harp and halo, rather just groping for a few quotable last words. The situation was growing more tense by the minute and they frankly revelled in it.

Of course, even the impending clash didn't keep us from nattering about the liver we had for supper. And surely that couldn't be Canadian bacon! But I wasn't complaining. At least I was back in a ship that had toilet tissue. Paper was so scarce in England that every tiny sheet of the roll I'd had to steal from the POs' heads in the *Duke of York* was stamped

'Government Property'! I thought we were invading very comfortably.

Lieutenant-Commander Denis Glover, DSC, of the Royal New Zealand Navy, described his one-man's-eye view of the main invasion fleet making for France on D-Day, 6 June 1944, in *Penguin New Writing No. 23*. For Hitler, what Glover saw was the beginning of the end.

The flotilla made a grand sight, steaming down to the open sea, threading its way in line ahead through the massed transports, crowded with men and vehicles that lay at anchor in the landlocked roadstead. In the grey evening could be smelt and felt the fresh tang of the Channel in one of its boisterous, threatening moods. The Commandos on deck looked round at the unfamiliar scene, at the waters they had exercised in so often. They were cheerful but restrained. There was the island, there the spit. The mainland lay on the quarter, misty, indistinct, in the smoky setting sun. For many it would be the last sight of England.

I must close up a little. On this of all occasions our station-keeping must be perfect. *Steady on the stern of the next ahead, Cox'n.* What's that hoist? Good, the flotilla officer wants more revs. Let's do the thing in style; might be our last gesture. The unknown morrow lies over our bows. They're cheering us from the transports. 'Give 'em hell!' I expect we all feel how few we are, how small and very much alone. Being cheered makes one feel heroic in a grand and desperate way. We assault early, but the transports will be there soon enough. We're all in this.

Now's the time for our signature tune over the loudhailer. *Switch on, Signalman.* Impudent and cheerful. But what's that? The pipes. Damn it, that's the brigadier's own piper on the fo'c'sle of the flotilla leader. The pipes are best. Mine sounds strident, flauntingly casual about the prospect of death, too flamboyant a gesture – but the pipes, the pipes are striking, fittest music for the fight. *Number One, why isn't that man wearing a lifebelt? Does he think this is a bloody picnic?*

Pray now for luck. The colonel and all these Commandos, battle-skilled and tough, putting themselves irrevocably into the hands of an amateur sailor. Well, I'll land these troops if it's the last thing I ever do – probably will be – I'll fight this ship till the guns fall off. Land them, if the whole crew lies dead on the deck. Oh, don't indulge in such silly private dramatics with yourself! *I say, Number One, ask the Middy to organise some cocoa.*

'Look here, you chaps,' said the flotilla officer at that last briefing, 'we won't let the Commandos down. We know these troops, we've trained with them, and we think a hell of a lot of them. We can't and won't let them down. We've only got two things to do. First, find the place over there, then put them ashore at all costs. What if we don't find exactly the right place? Don't start looking for it; land the troops at all costs.'

Port lookout! Keep your eyes open for a light on the port bow. By my reckoning it should have showed up by now. *Cox'n, how's your head?* South twenty east. And I estimate it should be south eleven east. But we can't steer to within ten degrees in this sea. All the same, don't want to end up in Le Havre – we'd look damn silly making an invasion by ourselves. Where in the hell are all those buoys? I haven't seen one yet, and by dead reckoning we've passed at least four. But how can you find buoys, or even lay them, in a sea like this? What a night – dark and wet, with just the sort of sea that makes the old tub wallow like a lovesick hippopotamus. All right for sailors, but I'm thinking about the troops. A lot sick already and half the rest in a stupor. They'll need their strength tomorrow, every ounce of it. I wish to hell I felt certain, absolutely certain, of our exact position. We're too much to the east. They said to avoid easting, emphatically. Wonder if I ought to signal up the line. No, Rupert knows what he's doing, though I wouldn't allow so much for wind myself. Funny, I thought there'd be lots of traffic about, and we haven't seen a single thing. Of course, we land pretty early, and are faster than most.

My God! Just these twelve small ships, and all these precious lives, alone in mid-Channel. Query, are lives precious in wartime? Yes, until they can be thrown away for their planned objective. *Hello, Colonel, come up on the bridge.* I wonder how he feels. *How are we getting on? Oh, fine, sir. Right up to time. We'll hit the run-in position in approximately three hours twenty minutes.* Either that or Le Havre harbour boom. Wacko, Rupert's spotted a dan buoy and altered course. That's better, south five east. *You see, sir, everything weighed off! Buoys laid to mark every channel – can't go wrong! No, the RNVR hasn't done badly in this war. Do you know, there isn't a single RN officer with us. Navigation? That's no worry – it's your seasick troops I'm worried about.* Yes, south five east, that allows for too much easting, and brings us back to my mean course of south eleven east. Navigating all of us to death, that's what I may be doing. To hell, I'm getting my head down for a while now Number One's been called. *Hello, Fritz. Good sleep? Course south five east, position about thirty miles from the run-in. Don't close up too much in this sea. Call me in two hours' time—till then for nothing less than an enemy destroyer!*

Reluctant dawn drew up the curtain on a grey and heaving sea, turning fantasies to spray-drenched reality. Far ahead gunfire rumbled and rolled, and the flashes were echoed faintly on the low cloud. Overhead through it swift squadrons raced southward. Dan buoys appeared, floating soddenly, their marker flags drowned and bedraggled. The deck of the next ahead plunged wetly through the seas; the next astern, who cheerily signalled 'Good bloody morning', yawed and rolled on its course. The flotilla drove steadily on. One or two Commandos, who had elected to sleep on deck all night, damply unrolled themselves, sat up, and shivered with the cold. This was the awaited dawn, fatal or glorious, heralded by guns.

Those flashes come from battle-wagons. Too deliberate a fire, too deep a roar, for anything smaller. *Bearing red one five? Very good, lookout.* Yes, there she is, and another beyond her. We're not a mile to the east, if they're in their bombardment positions. There they go again, now wait for the sound to reach us. Something mighty reassuring about battle-wagons. War elephants of the fleet, unhurried and packing a wallop. Destroyers rush about, guns barking like frenzied sheepdogs. And cruisers slide swiftly, specialists in pretty shooting, the accurate placing of sweet salvos. But the battlewagon – her great guns swing up in a silent arc. Then woof! with a sheet of flame that hides the ship she's hurled a packet of one-ton bricks at something out of sight. Then she stops to think for a while, and the ginger smoke rolls lazily away. Woof! again. The first for your concrete wall; now for your bathroom window. *Colonel, I once saw a sixteen-inch gun blow a perfect and gigantic smoke ring. I half expected the gun to waggle with pleasure, but it took absolutely no notice.* Now what's Rupert altering away westward for? Ah, yes, run-in position. *Yes, lookout, I see them.* There they are, huddled together on the skyline, a lot of ships, too. Lowering position for the assault craft, just like putting perambulators off a bus. *What's that, Colonel? Call you when we sight the beach – you know just what it looks like? Yes, sir, I'll do that. It'll be at least an hour yet.* This is where the old heart goes thump, thump in that heavy way. One more hour of uncertainty in which the chill finger of foreboding lays itself across my brow. Hm, line for a tragedy king. *How d'you feel, Middy? Myself, I wouldn't be elsewhere for a thousand quid. Well, not for a hundred anyway.* It's a comforting show of ships. We're not alone any more. Eight miles from them to the enemy, and just listen to the gunfire. All the mad dogs of hell barking over a bone on the beach, the invisible beach; and the shattering roll of the bombs. These ships are all too close together, if they're under fire themselves. *There's a wreck, port lookout, only her bows showing. Why the hell didn't you report it?*

Those assault carrier ships look like wolves meditating the attack. Some of their craft will have gone in by now. Small targets, but desperate business in this running surf. Some, maybe many, will be lost, but the rest will swarm on like sea-lice. We ignore this friendly company of ships, and go straight on. Perhaps the admiral there will note with approval that we are dead on time. Our job is by ourselves, a vital job, a king-pin job in the involved machinery of this invasion. *Well, Cox'n, you're a lucky man. Not everyone gets paid for taking a trip to the Continent! What? You'd sooner go to Blackpool?* Visibility is poor. At what distance will we sight that flat and fatal coast? In good time, I hope, to make any necessary alteration of course. Past the lowering position now, and off into the unknown. Nobody takes any notice. We'll show them. *Number One, old boy, we are altering to south seventeen west. Eight miles to go, and the revs up to 1400.* Good old ship, she runs her sweetest at 1400, and still 600 in reserve. *No, Middy, the gunners may not, repeat not, open fire if they see a submarine. Nor at anything else unless they're told. It is considered bad form to shoot down Spitfires.* This is exhilarating, this is exultantly fine. Never felt more aware, more full of life – if it weren't for that unpleasant tight feeling round the heart.

What did I say to Frank when we toasted ourselves the other day after those few drinks? Steer for the sound of the guns! Very dramatic, but the guns happen to be all round us, and all ours as far as I can make out. Hello, splashes. Not all ours then. That destroyer is firing as if it's had a fit, yes, and someone's been badly knocked about over there. Can't worry, it's a good gamble. We get hit or we don't get hit. Shell-fire you can't do anything about, but damned if I can feel happy about machine-guns on the beach. Here I am, conning a shipload of 104 hefty Commandos, fifteen seamen and two officers of my own, running on a timetable towards terror. And there are 4000 gallons of high-octane petrol under my deck. Wonder how they feel in the engine room where they can't even see what's going on, just trust in me and hope like hell. I shall light another pipe.

The silhouettes and scale models in the intelligence room looked like toys out of an expensive nursery. It was all there – the canal entrance, the scattered town along the shore, the church spire, the chateau by the wood, the pill-box, trench, strong-point, emplacement, emplacement, emplacement. Stretching seaward over the flat tidal beach the rows of posts, stakes, spikes and mines bristling like a hedgehog. 'Your parking beach,' said the naval intelligence officer, 'is 800 yards long. Its limit on the east is this modern villa by the road, on the west these two distinctive steep-roofed houses. To the west it doesn't matter much – you may get in the way of others, but land anywhere if you must. But to the east, not one yard beyond your limit.' He smiled cheerfully. 'Not that any of these buildings are likely to be standing by the time the Navy and the RAF have got going. All you can expect is smoke and fire and haze and maybe a helpful pile of rubble.' He spoke perfect English for a Frenchman, and knew so much he might have been on that beach for the past few months. He probably had.

There it is, the flat, sleeping coast, charged with peril. Ships, warships, lie all round us. Their guns are going all the time. I like the way they've comfortably dropped their hooks as if they've come to settle down. *Disappointing from a tourist's point of view, Number One* – why must I give way to this affectation of flippancy? – *but call the colonel: he wants to view the promised land.* How good our ships look. Small, but purposeful. They were built for this hour. There's a signal hoist – how many have I watched from that same yard-arm? – division, church, order zero: assume arrowhead formation when executived. There's Jack astern looking at me through his glasses just as I look at him through mine. *I'll* be very funny indeed and raise my cap with extravagant politeness!

That's surely the château, Colonel, through the smoke. A cable to starboard of it is our limit. Can you see the modern villa? Not there. That should be it, sir, that white ruin, what do you think? Good, bang on the right beach. We've been steering a lot more west than seventeen too. Good old Rupert, good old all of us! Not far to go, and anywhere in the 800 yards to the west of the ruin. Any minute, every ship for itself.

Now eyes for everything, eyes for nothing. The beach looms close, maybe a mile. There are people running up and down it. There are fires, and the bursting of shells. Yes, and wrecked landing craft everywhere, a flurry of propellers in the savage surf and among those wicked obstructions. Beach-clearance parties, I expect, bloody heroes, every one. Special craft stooging quietly in, some of them on fire, though. Diesel fuel burns black. That vicious destroyer to port is irritating me, but the colonel doesn't seem to mind. He's cool but I bet he's worried. Curious how all these soldiers dislike an assault by water. I'd hate to dash out of foxholes at machine-guns. Damn him, I can pretend I'm cool, too. *It's the noisiest gun – starboard ten! – it's the noisiest gun in the Navy, that four point seven – Midships, Cox'n!* What a cool, disinterested reply he makes. Colonel, you make me grin. I like your nerve.

We are on those bristling stakes. They stretch before us in rows. The mines on them look as big as planets. And those graze-nose shells pointing towards us on some of them look like beer bottles. Oh, God, I *would* be blown up on a mine like a beer bottle! Now for speed and skill and concentration. Whang, here it comes – those whizzing ones will be mortars – and the stuff is falling all round us. Can't avoid them, but the mines and collisions I can avoid. Speed, more speed. Put them off by speed, weave in and out of these bloody spikes, avoid the mines, avoid our friends, avoid the wrecked craft and vehicles in the rising water, and *get these troops ashore*. Good, the Commando officers have their men ready and waiting, crouched along the decks. Number One is for'ard with his ramp parties ready. Everything is working as we've exercised it for so long. Oh, hell, this new tin hat is far too big for me – I'll shake it off my head out of fright if I'm not careful. *Port twenty. Midships. Starboard ten*. That was a near one. Nearly hit it. But we won't, we can't, slow down. *Midships. Port ten, port fifteen, port twenty*. We're going to hit it, we're going to hit it! A beer bottle, I knew it. *Ease to ten. Midships!* Not bows on, though. We'll strike to starboard on the beam. One, two, three, four, five.... Huh, nothing's happened. Must be luck for me in beer bottles after all. Now for the next lot of obstructions.

Don't jump, you fool. It was near, but you're not hit. Straddled. All right, keep on. And here's where I go in, that little bit of clear beach. *Port ten. Midships. Starboard five*. Wish the swell weren't throwing us about so much. Let's be in first, as a glorious gesture, then no one will know how frightened we really were. Tommy always said when coaching us: If you hang around on the outside of the scrum you'll get hurt – go in! *Sorry to give you so much work, Cox'n*. That'll rock him, and I'll light up my pipe, too. What does he say? Nae bother at all, sir, and I'm still sticking to my pipe, am I? Can't even the enemy take the bounce out of this, Cox'n? *You're not being familiar, I hope, Cox'n?* I mustn't grin. What? Not bloody likely? Anyhow, he's a cocky bastard and cheerful. A shell may kill us both any minute.

Slow ahead together. Slow down to steady the ship, point her as you want her, then half ahead together and on to the beach with a gathering rush. Put her ashore and be damned! She's touched down. One more good shove ahead to wedge her firm. *Out ramps!*

Smooth work, Fitz, oh, smooth as clockwork. *Now off you go! Good luck, Commandos, go like hell! Next meeting – Brighton!* How efficiently, how quickly, they run down the accustomed ramps, not a man hit that I can see, and there they go splashing through a hundred yards of water, up over more of the flat beach than that, and out of sight among the deadly dunes. The colonel turns to wave, and is gone with them. They ignore beach fire. They have their objective and they are going for it, the best troops we can produce. God be with them.

Rupert's decks were clear before ours after all, there he is to port. And now here's Woodie beside me to starboard. And Chris and Jack grounded on my port quarter. Good work, oh, good for us! *Number One, in ramps! Come on, get those bloody ramps IN!* None of the crew hit yet that I can see. Let's get out quick. Any of our craft hit? Yes, there's Les – seems to be on fire aft, but quite unperturbed. And Chris has a lot of confusion on his fo'c'sle. Casualties. How can I get out with him across my stern? *Middy, take the depth aft.*

Christ, that's too near! Don't want to be killed now. Mortar, fifteen yards. Little bits rattling against the bridge. And a nasty concentration on the beach. How slowly men spin before they fall. Some look surprised as they die. Oh, come on, Chris! Who's that damn fool opening up with a machine-gun past my bridge? Minor craft astern, I suppose. As if there isn't enough to put up with. No! It's coming from ashore! *Port gunner! Tall building bearing red one five, red one five. Fire!* Hah, quick-triggered, that boy, oh, and lovely shooting: a stream of tracer from both guns hose-piping on every window. Don't you take us on with a machine-gun, Jerry. You'll get hot porridge back. No return fire, anyway. Hope we got the bastard.

Right. *Half astern together.* We're off. Must avoid incoming craft as well as dodge those stakes. Damn, she never would steer coming astern. We hit that one. Never mind, the mines are all set on the seaward side. Turn short round. *That's that, Fitz. Now we'll take a look round. I say! Those aren't chance shots. They're stalking us out to sea!* Splash to starboard, splash to port, ahead, astern. Now I'm in a rage, full of exultation, fear, contempt, intoxication with the hour and the day. Does that damned Jerry think he can hit us going out when he couldn't hit us coming in? Wasting time on an empty ship when the beach is full of targets! Of course, he just might. . . . Good shooting, oh, very nice. But now I've landed my troops it's ME you're taking on. *Cox'n, steer for that last burst.* Bet he can't put one on the same spot twice.

Hell! What an explosion! And, my God, it's one of ours! *Fitz, who is it, who is it?* Must have been hit in the tanks. God, oh God, poor bastards! *No, we're too far away. Others are going in.* There won't be a man alive when the smoke clears. But they landed their troops at all costs. At all costs. And blown up coming off. Who's that over there, bows up and sinking? Stan. I can read his number. Abandoned, I think. *Signalman, call her up. Take a look, Number One. I think she's abandoned. Yes?* This area is warming up. Surely the fire is faster and better than it was? Jerry is a stubborn bastard. The landing has been made, and the others are coming in wave upon wave. Now, why the hell must he keep on firing at me?

On the beaches the opposition intensified in many places some hours after the initial assault. The Germans went to earth to fight, using cunning where force had failed. Guns and mortars ranged the landing areas with precision, the sniping was deadly and persistent. But still the assault went on, till the shallow water was crammed with twisted metal wreckage, blazing vehicles and disabled craft. Still the assault went on, and the troops were put ashore with the inevitability of the rising tide that covered the beach obstructions and made navigation more perilous than before.

Who's that hailing us? Yes, that infantry landing craft. Full of troops. She's been hit. Listing badly. Sinking, I should say. *LCI(L), LCI(L), I am coming alongside. That's right, Number One, all the fenders you've got. We'll get a bashing in this swell. Give the lines plenty of scope.* Holed on the waterline, she is. I think she'll last, though. Don't like these shells falling round, but it's worse for the pongos, and them still seasick. *Bad luck, chum! But we'll run the ferry service. All aboard for Margate!* Damn silly to shout such rubbish, but it may sound confident. Hell, I don't want to go into that bloody beach again.

Come on, lads, help them aboard, and ALL their equipment. Now, wait for it, there, wait till she rolls towards you, THEN jump. This is going to take time. Horrible being hoveto under fire. Honest, I'm in a worse funk than the first time. Because of that gun that seems told off to get us. Surely it will be easier on the beaches by now. *Casualties? Sure, we'll take them for you. Number One, Cox'n, get them aboard and do what you can. Hello, Major, now where can I take you? Oh, I know where it is: nothing's a trouble.* Bad luck being smashed up before they've landed, but what a load – twice as many as we should take. One hit and this crowded deck will look like a butcher's shop. Troops don't know the craft either. Slow getting on means slower getting off. And all that equipment! Commandos move fast because they're light. Well, in we go again. *Cox'n, steady on the gap between those two buildings ashore. See them? Right.*

This is being under fire in real earnest. Or am I more nervous than I was? We'll pick our way between the bursts, swerving nicely, duck when we hear a mortar, and keep our fingers crossed. *Starboard ten. Midships.* Nearly didn't see that sunk tank or whatever it was. Too many new fires on that beach, and small-arms shooting, too. Hope it's us cleaning up. *Yes, Major, that's it ahead. We've been surf-riding round here all morning. The beach is ours all right. It's just like home to half the army now.*

Good old Fitz. He's standing by to beach as if we were running a London bus. And the crew were lounging as if they'd been under fire for weeks. Showing off in front of these pongos – good. Don't expect they've been through it before, and they're seasick as well. Ah, another row of obstructions. There should be more like these, totally submerged. Horrible to be wrecked now. But take a chance — I'm going in here, and going in fast.

Out ramps! And there goes one right overboard. Preventer stay gone. *All right, you troops, now get off on the other one. Take it easy, but get off, and DON'T leave your equipment behind you.* Nothing to do but wait. And there are more explosions, beach mines, bodies, going up. Men and machines tossed in the air. And that mortar is killing people. Too damned near, and the tank beyond our bows blazing like hell.

Oh, for Pete's sake, why must this big landing craft come in so close to me? His kedge-wire will be hard to miss, and if I go to port I may crash on the wreck there. *Come on, troops, get OFF! Throw that equipment down to them, you, for'ard. No, NOT in the water.* The men are coming off this next craft. And on to a mine, not twenty yards from our bows. Here's another mortar. *Duck!* Hell, right on her fo'c'sle. If she hadn't come so close we would have stopped that one. Oh, I don't like this at all. *Number One, are those troops getting off?*

Off at last! And still not hit, by some good luck, except for the rattle of fragments on the deck. Some of our troops hit, though. Silly bastards, they should have got up that beach and away, instead of milling around. Now out to sea, Harry Flatters. *See any more of our craft, Signalman?* Thank God. I've had enough of this for a while. After how many mathematical probabilities does one run into a shell while trying to dodge them? *Two thousand revs, Cox'n, steer north fifteen east.* We must rendezvous. Heaven knows what's happened to the flotilla. *I say, Number One, we're two miles out and still being shelled. Persistent sods, aren't they?*

So it is. That's Joe's craft. What's he doing as far out as this and sinking, too? He can't last long — screws out of the water and blowing down on the uncleared mines. *Starboard ten. We'd better close him.* Now what earthly good do those stupid Jerries think they're doing by trying to shell a sinking ship? *Flash him, Signalman. Will take you off.* OK, Joe, we're

107

coming. *No, Fitz, he's past towing. Too far gone. We won't be any too soon.*

Hiyah, Joe! I'm coming alongside. Got all your crew there? Underwater damage, I guess. Yes, there's a bloody great hole midships. Silly those propellers look sticking uselessly out of the water. *What's that, Joe? Told you to beach yourself in shallow water? Eh? You said you would if you were a bloody Spitfire?* Good old Joe. Perhaps I'm jumpy, but I'm not putting out lines. She looks as if she'll nose-dive any minute. Crash alongside, and get them over. We may still stop a packet. *All aboard?* Yes, she's lurching now. Poor Joe. Nobody wants to see a ship go down, let alone his own. *Well, Joe, if that's Jerry's Atlantic Wall I don't think much of it. What? Just shows you can't trust no bastard, does it?* Good old Joe, that's right in character.

Number One, we will now get to seaward out of here, and find the rest. Issue rum to everybody. And, my God, I'll have a tot myself!

12 Attack!

Edward Young

While the Army fought its final battles in Europe, there was still plenty for the Navy to do, not only in the Atlantic and home waters, but also against the Japanese in the Pacific, where the Americans were slowly pushing the enemy back. During September 1944 Commander Edward Young, DSO, DSC, found himself forced to use his submarine as a surface warship against Japanese vessels working among the islands off southern Burma.

It was not until half past nine that morning that we saw the head of the convoy emerging from the inner channel exactly where I had expected. As on the previous day, it was a long time – about an hour and a half – before the slow-moving ships reached our position. In the intervals of watching them through the periscope I studied the chart and memorised the general shape of the sea's bottom so that I had a fairly accurate mental picture of the shoal dangers. I knew that once the action started there would be no opportunity of precise fixing and that this would be another case of navigating by eye.

Beyond deciding to let all the ships pass me before surfacing, hoping thus to minimise the chances of a massed ramming attack, I still could not make up my mind what tactics to adopt. Submarines had never been designed for this sort of work, and I had a strong foreboding that the odds were weighted too heavily against us. But we could not sit tamely there and watch them pass unharmed. We must *do* something.

Once again I had to contend with a sea that was as unruffled as a sheet of polished glass. It was desperate work trying to keep track of the movements of so many ships with only split-second observations through the periscope. The two escorts seemed very much aware that they were approaching a danger point, for they were moving in a rapid and continuous zigzag on the seaward beam of the convoy. However, although they passed within about 200 yards of us, they did not spot the periscope, and when the second of them was well past us we were abeam of the last coaster of the column. Now, if ever, was the moment for gun action.

When I gave the order to surface it was the first time I had ever done so without knowing exactly what I meant to do when I got to the top. Climbing the ladder to the bridge on the heels of the gun's crew, I was in a blue funk and full of a premonition of disaster.

Yet as soon as I reached the bridge and stood in the sunshine under the blue sky all my apprehensions were miraculously swept away. Every one of our guns opened fire at once without a hitch and continued firing for the next thirty-six minutes without any of the stoppages which had sometimes let us down in the past. Action, once joined, produced its own stimulus to the brain; our tactics were adapted every moment to meet the changing situation, and we were never at a loss.

11.17 Opened fire at the rear ship at a range of 2000 yards, obtaining seven or eight fairly destructive hits. She turned away and limped towards the shore. We then attacked and stopped the ship ahead of her, but both the escorts were now racing towards us, firing their machine-guns. Turned to port to bring them both on to the starboard bow, and directed the fire of all our guns on to them. In turn they were each hit and stopped by several direct hits from the three-inch. This part of the action was most exciting, the range eventually closing to 400 yards. The enemy were very brave, and we were lucky not to suffer any casualties. Both these escorts were carrying a score or so of Japanese, presumably troops.

One of them released a depth-charge (or it may have been shot over the side) when it was 500 yards away, and it went off on the bottom causing the submarine to heel slightly to starboard for a moment. One of the escorts got out of control, and eventually drove herself under, still with way on. The other remained afloat and was sunk later when things calmed down.

In the meantime, a small vessel had been sighted approaching from the northward at great speed. This looked too much like a motor torpedo boat to be healthy, so it was the next target to be engaged. At the same time a constant-helm zigzag was maintained. Several near-misses were seen before the torpedo boat, at a range of about 3000 yards, turned and fired two stern torpedoes. The tracks passed about 100 yards astern of us. One definite direct hit was scored on this MTB as she was retiring, at a range of about 4000 yards, and she took little further interest in the proceedings. I think our shooting had put her off quite effectively.

Before this, some vessel had opened up with a pompom. We traced the firing to a small ship not previously sighted which lay stopped about 4000 yards away, and began to get uncomfortably accurate. Fortunately this fellow, probably a motor gunboat, obtained only one direct hit, which struck *Storm*'s bridge casing below the Oerlikon and caused no casualties. Neither the motor torpedo boat nor the gunboat had been previously seen through the periscope, and it is considered that they came out from Mergui to meet the convoy.

All this time, also, there was a perpetual whine of machine-gun bullets, but it was difficult to see exactly which ships were firing. They caused no casualties. It was now decided to finish off the coaster which had been stopped earlier (the second target engaged) and also the other escort. These both sank after a few short-range waterline shots. Meanwhile, the first coaster we had attacked and severely damaged appeared to have beached herself; later, however, she seemed to be still under way and may have succeeded in proceeding with the remainder. Fire was now directed at a coaster which had stopped about 4000 yards away. Two direct hits were obtained, and his bridge demolished.

But by this time we had fired over 150 rounds of three-inch and the barrel was so heated that the next round jammed. Moreover, the remainder of the convoy was getting out of range, we had exhausted all our pans of Oerlikon and Vickers ammunition, and I was getting anxious about the navigation. I decided to call it a day, as the situation did not justify the risk of running the submarine aground.

11.53 Broke off the action and retired westward on the surface, passing through the gap north of Bentinck Island. There seemed no point in remaining in the vicinity.

The net result of the action was: two escorts and one coaster sunk, two coasters damaged, one torpedo boat hit. Also, the last clue to the inshore convoy route had been uncovered. An interesting point was that all the survivors seen in the water were apparently Japanese. Not a single Malay or Burman was among them, though these had been plentiful in the coasters sunk on the previous patrol.

I was staggered, and profoundly thankful, that we had survived those thirty-six minutes without a single casualty. There was great elation throughout the boat at our success. The gun's crew were no doubt regaling their messmates below with vivid descriptions of the action; they had enjoyed themselves, and were only too disappointed when the engagement was broken off. Inspired by the grim determination of Taylor, the gun-layer, they had done very well, quite unperturbed by the machine-gun fire coming at us from all directions; even Greenway, now back in the gun's crew as breach-worker, was unshaken by any memories of his previous wounding in somewhat similar circumstances. My highest admiration went to Richard Blake, who as gunnery control officer had been faced with unusually rapid decisions – for my constant shifts of target, and the wild zigzag forced on us by the threat of torpedoes from the MTB had demanded frequent and immediate corrections to range and deflection. In spite of these difficulties he had remained cool, patient and accurate. At the end both he and I were hoarse from shouting our orders above the inferno of noise. For several hours afterwards we were partially deaf, and I think it must have been on this occasion that Blake suffered the damage to his eardrums which led, five years after the end of the war, to his being invalided out of the service...

Out of the original nine ships we had sunk three and damaged two. It was better than I had hoped for when we surfaced, but I could not help remembering that if I had been quicker on the uptake on the previous day we should probably have taken a heavier toll and might even have sunk the entire convoy.

13 Suicide pilots

Officers of HMS 'Formidable'

As the war against Japan progressed in 1945, this ever-surprising enemy produced a weapon that astonished Allied sailors. This was the 'Divine Wind', the Kamikaze – suicide pilots who deliberately crashed their explosive-laden airplanes into the decks of Allied warships. These young pilots, many of them hardly able to fly, believed themselves to be on a religious mission in defence of their country. They were sent to their certain deaths with much ceremony and were considered heroes by their countrymen.

Once locked into their planes they flew directly to their targets and crash-dived into their chosen ships. Many of these human bombs were brought down by fighter planes or anti-aircraft guns before they could cause damage; but many survived the withering defence put up by the Allies and wreaked havoc aboard the ships they hit. The Kamikaze was a last desperate gesture of a beaten aggressor.

HMS *Formidable* suffered an attack of the 'Divine Wind' on 4 May 1945 during the Allied invasion of the island of Okinawa.

Suddenly, without any warning, there was the fierce 'whoosh' of an aircraft passing very fast and low overhead, and I looked up in time to see a fighter plane climbing away on the starboard bow, having crossed the deck from port at about fifty feet. I was thinking casually what a stupid thing it was to do and, at the present juncture, how lucky he was not to have been shot at, when the starboard bow Oerlikons opened up with a stream of tracer. The plane banked steeply. I saw the red blobs of its Japanese markings. Pompoms joined the Oerlikons and it flew down the starboard side of the ship, the focus of a huge cone of converging tracer. I thought he was certain to 'buy it' and stood watching until he passed behind the island. The noise of the close-range weapons drowned the engines of the taxi-ing aircraft.

Then the Japanese plane came into sight again from behind the island, banking hard to close the ship over the starboard quarter. He was still apparently unharmed and now, out astern, the target of fewer guns; for fewer could be brought to bear at that angle, a fact he probably knew. His silhouette changed to a thin line with a bulge in the middle and he seemed to hang in the air as he dived for the ship.

I had waited long enough and ran about fifteen yards forward to a hatch, down which I jumped in the company of a rather fat leading seaman. As we hit the deck an immense crash shook the ship. I gave it a second or two to subside, during which the light from above changed to bright orange, and ran up again.

It was a grim sight. A fire was blazing among wreckage close under the bridge, flames reached up the side of the island and clouds of black smoke billowed far above the ship. Much of the smoke came from the fires on deck but as much seemed to be issuing from the funnel and this for the moment gave the impression of damage deep below decks. The bridge windows seemed to gape like eye sockets and much of the superstructure was blackened. The deck was littered with debris, much of it on fire, and there was not a soul to be seen.

Men soon poured up from the side of the deck and the work began. The main fire was very fierce and occasional machine-gun bullets 'cooked-off'. The smell of fire mingled with the indescribably disgusting smell of the foam-compound. Subsidiary fires in the tow-motor park, fire-fighting headquarters (!) and elsewhere were attacked by hand extinguishers. Unburnt aircraft were pushed clear, casualties were carried below, and after about half an hour everything was under control. Additional hands and foam-compound arrived from below and large pieces of smouldering wreckage were ditched by crane.

The Kamikaze which hit us had carried a 500 lb bomb and it is thought the pilot released it just before he struck.

A slice of bomb about 1 ft by 9 in. by 4 in. went straight downwards and came to rest in a fuel tank. On its way it buckled a hangar fire curtain and penetrated an emergency steam pipe which filled the centre boiler room with steam; one or two valves had to be turned very promptly before that space was left to the scalding steam. It was this large and persistent splinter which was responsible for the volumes of black smoke and the thin white streamer of steam from the funnel, and for the reduction of our speed to eighteen knots. The work of filling the hole with steel plate and rapid-hardening cement and of making one aircraft carrier work by hand tackle began, and the repair of damaged electrical, radar and signalling equipment was put in hand. By 17.00 these and machinery repairs were to be so far advanced that the captain could tell his admiral that we were capable of twenty-four knots and of landing-on our aircraft.

When one considers the appearance of the deck immediately after the incident our casualties seemed comparatively light. Two officers and six men were killed and six officers and forty-one men wounded.

One Avenger – its pilot and the petty officer directing it died of their wounds later – blew up with the Kamikaze and seven other aircraft on deck were completely burnt out. Other aircraft on deck were damaged. All the small tractors were destroyed, and aircraft thereafter had to be moved by man- and jeep-power.

The fact that the Japanese pilot coldly decided his aim was not good enough and went round again points to a high standard of training among suicide pilots. This fellow dealt with himself very thoroughly, too, for he scattered his pieces all over the place. The wristwatch found far away on one of his hands had stopped and the gunnery officer was at one stage seen poking pieces of him off the funnel with a long stick.

14 Surrender

Anthony Kimmins

The war with Japan finished at 12.00 on 15 August 1945. Commander Anthony Kimmins, OBE, RN, witnessed the moment when Hong Kong was returned to British rule, and told the story in his book *Half Time*. The long-awaited end had come.

As we arrived off the coast of China we were still completely in the dark as to what attitude the Japanese troops were adopting, and whether they were obeying the Emperor's instructions to lay down their arms. We also had very little information as to the position of minefields.

Admiral Harcourt decided to lie off the coast for a time while efforts were made to get in touch with the Japanese by radio. At last the following message was received:

'To any British man o' war. From Hong Kong, Japan. To the Chief of the Communications Corps of the British Squadron off Hong Kong from Y. Kawato, lieutenant, the Chief of the Communications Corps of the Japanese Army.

'One: Congratulations for the commencement of the wireless communication between your squadron and our corps.

'Two: Our location is Two Three Seven Queen Mary Road, Kowloon.

'Three: We want to know the name and rank of you, the name of the ship and the location of it.

'Four: We hope that the friendly and smoothly communication should be continued between us for ever.'

This was followed almost immediately by a request to send an aircraft to Kai-Tak aerodrome to bring off a Japanese envoy and Commander Craven, the senior British naval prisoner. Douglas Craven, a term-mate of mine at Osborne and Dartmouth, had made a special name for himself in the Navy as a brilliant amateur jockey, and in the past had always had difficulty in keeping his weight down, but as he stepped out on to the flight deck of the *Indomitable*, almost straight from a long stretch of solitary confinement, he could have ridden as bottom weight anywhere. But in spite of being so weak, he braced his shoulders and saluted just as smartly as if he had been on parade at the gunnery school. Here was the moment he must have prayed for again and again during those interminable minutes, days, nights, weeks, months and years, but he never said a word of all that. He was back on the job, a staff officer with important information regarding future events. As I followed those two matchsticks of legs up the ladder to the admiral's sea cabin there was something about the polish which he had given to what was left of his shoes that made me proud to belong to the same Service.

Later that evening – after Craven had finished his discussions with the admiral – I took him down to the wardroom. This was the moment, I felt sure, when he would explode with pent-up relief. He could have what he liked – beer, whisky, gin – he only had to say the word. I searched eagerly for the look of excitement in his eyes, but it was too early yet. They seemed unable to focus. They were still numbed by countless hours of staring at a blank wall only a few feet away. He politely accepted a glass of beer, but the noise and crowded room were obviously too much for him. I was just about to take him away to a quieter spot when a New Zealander – the one man who had escaped from the prison camp where Douglas Craven had been senior naval officer – came in.

There was something almost uncanny about the way those two shook hands and looked into each other's eyes.

'We never heard, of course,' said Craven, 'but I was always certain you'd get through.'

Goodwin didn't answer for a moment.

'My one worry was reprisals. I heard a rumour that you'd been executed.'

I crept quietly away. It seemed the most offensive form of eavesdropping, as if one were listening in to two men who belonged to another world.

More TOPLINERS for your enjoyment

One of the Gang
Dick Cate
Five stories about life among the coal pits of Durham: Dick Cate remembers being football crazy; joining every gang and group that was going, from the Boys' Brigade to the church choir; fighting off the Gladstoners; coming face to face with the bully Starkey; and how his Uncle Jack found a place in the sun at last. By the author of the popular Topliner, *On the Run*, this is another incident-packed, fast moving and funny collection.

The Topliner Book of Coarse Fishing
John Goodwin
All you need to know to start out in Britain's most popular sport – the gear, the fish, the best (and the worst) ways of catching them, the competition, and the lazy Sunday afternoons. There are lots of clear illustrations and diagrams showing what to look for when you're buying tackle – and what to do with it when you've got it!

Joey's Room
Geraldine Kaye
After Joey's death, his younger sister discovers his room, where he lived away from the family. With it, she finds a world she didn't know existed – full of fresh ideas, and people who live by different standards from her parents. Another popular Topliner by the author of *Marie Alone*.

And also available in TOPLINER REDSTARS

King Caliban and other stories
John Wain
There's big money to be made in the wrestling ring. Fred might not be very bright, but he is big. Enormous, in fact. And he needs money. So, enter King Caliban, the unexpected terror of the ring. One of five stories about people on the brink of adulthood, by one of our leading poets and novelists. With a new introduction specially written for Redstars, in which John Wain remembers himself at sixteen, growing up during the last war.

TOPLINERS published by Macmillan

More TOPLINERS for your enjoyment

Fighters in the Sky
Aidan Chambers
More true stories from the Second World War. Real-life adventures of the men who took part in the war high above the ground.

Men at War
Aidan Chambers
True stories from the Second World War about the men who fought the war on land. Told in their own words this book shows the courage, excitement and thrills – the tragedy, the horror and the waste of war.

A Hitch on the Way
Philippa Adams
Hazards lie in wait when Judy sets off to hitch-hike to London, but none so surprising as old 'Gran' and her parrot...

The Girl in the Opposite Bed
Honor Arundel
Jane hates being in hospital, but by the time she goes home she knows much more about people – herself as well as others.

Siege at Robins Hill
Christine Dickenson
Awkward relatives, the Children's Department, even the police, cannot break Janice's resolve to keep her orphaned family together.

Us Boys of Westcroft
Petronella Breinburg
Walter Collins tells the story of his days at Westcroft School, where he's been sent as a last chance to set himself free from trouble, to start a new life.

Louie's SOS
E. W. Hildick
The case of the dirty milk bottles and how Louie's Lot rallied round.

TOPLINERS published by Macmillan

More TOPLINERS for your enjoyment

Who Wants to be a Dead Hero?
Adam King
When David's father is found dead, everyone believes it was an accident. But when David starts asking awkward questions, he finds himself involved in an international plot of mind-boggling dimensions.

The Pit
Reginald Maddock
Butch is determined to clear his name when accused of breaking into the school shop – even though it means facing the Pit to do so.

Is It Always Like This?
Ray Pope
When Pinky's gang find two little kids abandoned in their den, they decide to look after them until the parents are found. But doing that is a bigger problem than Pinky expected.

Break-In
Barry Pointon
Scared of being labelled 'chicken', Denton joins a gang at school, and trouble quickly follows.

East End at Your Feet
Farrukh Dhondy
Six stories about London teenagers from Asian and English families, and the problems of integrating the traditional values with those of a newer society, told with humour, compassion and insight into the lives of the young people involved.

The editor of Topliners is always pleased to hear what readers think of the books and to receive ideas for new titles. If you want to write to him please address your letter to: The Editor, Topliners, Macmillan, Little Essex Street, London WC2R 3LF. All letters received will be answered.

TOPLINERS published by Macmillan